365 feng shui tips

lillian too

365 feng shui tips

BARNES & NOBLE
NEW YORK

This 2006 edition published by Barnes & Noble Publishing, Inc. by arrangement with Ivy Press Limited.

This book was designed and produced by
Ixos Press an imprint of Ivy Press Limited
The Old Candlemakers
West Street, Lewes
East Sussex BN7 2NZ, UK
www.ivy-group.co.uk

Publisher: David Alexander
Creative Director: Peter Bridgewater
Art Director: Sarah Howerd
Editorial Director: Caroline Earle
Senior Project Editor: Rebecca Saraceno
Designer: Richard Constable
Illustrator: Jim Pilston
Picture Researcher: Anna Davies

2006 Barnes & Noble Publishing

ISBN-13: 978-07607-8307-8
ISBN-10: 0-7607-8307-1

Library of Congress Cataloging-in-Publication Data available

Printed and bound in China

1 3 5 7 9 10 8 6 4 2

Contents

Symbols key

home

work

wealth

love

luck

success

education

children

health

family

Introduction

This comprehensive little book of tips has come into fruition after numerous requests for a concise and accurate reference book for the practice of feng shui. The tips and cures contained within the following pages are easy to understand, simple to practice, and very effective in helping those new to feng shui get a feel for what it entails.

Feng shui is about living in awareness of the environment. Feng shui practice requires you to get acquainted with compass orientations that are implicit in the layout and elevations of all buildings. Homes and offices alike have facing and sitting directions that reflect the readings of the compass and it is these orientations that enable anyone to begin the business of creating good feng shui. Furthermore, feng shui is about shapes, forms, and structures so these are also factored into the whole feng shui "equation." How these equations work is based on how buildings, roads, rivers, and structures in the environment and everything placed in the living space interact with each other. These interactions have feng shui implications that are based on the theory of the five elements. These elements also have a yin and yang aspect.

The feng shui cures, suggestions, and advice that make up the tips in this book are based on feng shui equations and guidelines but they have been written to make feng shui instantly accessible. There are no lengthy explanations in this book. The tips are succinct, user-friendly, and coded with a symbol to show which topics are covered (the full list of symbols is shown on the contents page). There are 365 tips, one tip for each day of the year. For those wanting more detailed explanations and advice on the different formulas and aspects of feng shui practice, you might want to go online and visit www.wofs.com—the most comprehensive and extensive website on feng shui. It is also the most popular website on feng shui with feature articles on the theories and practice of all the different formulas and equations of feng shui. Let this book be a gentle introduction to this amazing practice. When you have checked out the suggestions contained here you might then want to go deeper and investigate more thoroughly how this ancient practice has been enjoying such a spectacular revival of interest. You will find that practicing feng shui is like applying an additional skill of living to your repertoire—it is neither spiritual nor religious. Instead, feng shui is a living skill—one well worth learning as it can bring better health, greater wealth, and much more happiness into your life.

Lillian Too

001 Good feng shui starts with good location

Auspicious locations are usually slightly elevated places where the "Green Dragon" on your left nestles gently with the "White Tiger" on your right, their bodies curving gently to create an armchair formation. The land is protected at the back by hills that symbolize the Black Tortoise, while in the South the presence of the Crimson Phoenix enhances the site. And if, facing this wonderful configuration of hills and mountains there is also a view of meandering or slow moving water; and if the vegetation in the area is also green and luscious, then placing your home here brings an abundance of good fortune. There will be enormous wealth for the household for succeeding generations. The first step is to try to find such a site.

002 Let the Dragon be higher than the Tiger

For good feng shui, the Dragon hills (or buildings if you live in the city) on your left should be slightly higher than the Tiger hills on your right, when you are looking inside looking out. If it is not, then a bright light should be installed to "lift the energy of the Dragon."

003 Always look for the symbolic Tortoise

The back of every house or building benefits from the "Tortoise effect"—Tortoise hills at the back should be rounded, indicating support. When the back Tortoise is missing, build a wall, plant some trees or better yet, place an artificial tortoise there to simulate the chi energy of this celestial creature. If you have a small water pond in your garden, it is very good feng shui to place some tortoises inside the pond. This creates longevity luck for the residents.

004 Create the bright hall effect

In front of the house, always endeavor to create a small level area because this creates the auspicious bright hall effect. This part of your home represents the Phoenix and this celestial bird benefits from an expanse of open space. The bright hall formation allows incoming chi to settle and turn benevolent before entering your home. If you place a bird of some kind somewhere in this part of the home, residents will benefit from many moneymaking opportunities.

005 Undulating land is superior

Gentle slopes are very auspicious and are superior to land that is completely flat. But also avoid land that is excessively steep. The ideal land is slightly higher behind and lower in front. Such land is said to have the potential to nurture Dragons.

006 Land with compact reddish soil brings abundance

Look for land that has compact reddish loam. Such soil is full of the breath of the Dragon, which is the celestial breath that brings abundance. Avoid hard rocky soil where even the grass cannot grow.

007 Find land with good fortune symbols

Look for hill formations that remind you of some good fortune symbol such as a dragon head, a coin, or a butterfly. If your land has a view of a "symbol" that appeals to you, then living there will bring you good fortune. On the other hand when hill formations or rock outcrops remind you of fierce predatory animals such as eagles, tigers, and even rats and foxes, these can bring misfortune and illness. Once in Hong Kong in the Sixties, an entire apartment block came sliding down in the Mid Levels, killing many of those living there. It was reported that feng shui masters had repeatedly warned of the outcrop of rock overhanging the apartment block. Some said it resembled a panther about to spring on the building—and it finally did. So do be alert to malevolent rock outcrops that seem to threaten your home or building. Might be better to move out.

008 Three peaks denote honors for children

When there are three vertical peaks within view of your house, it suggests that the children of the home will attain great academic honors. In China there is a legend that the late Supreme Leader Deng Hsiao Ping came from a house with just such a view—so his village had always expected that his family would produce a great scholar. They produced a great leader instead. You can simulate the presence of "three peaks" to benefit the scholastic aspirations of your children by using three peaks as a design on your wall or gate.

009 Placement of water is vital

Water can be artificially created and will be as effective as natural water. Where pools of water are man made they should be cleverly placed to tap into auspicious chi energy based on different formulas. Never try to create big bodies of water in your home without accurate compass feng shui input. There is nothing more dangerous. On the other hand, when water is correctly placed in accordance with any one of the formulas, then water has the capability of attracting serious wealth luck for you.

010 Water that is visible should be clean

To benefit the household residents, any kind of water that is visible from the house must be clean and flowing. Stagnant water is negative yin water and can be harmful to health. Yang water is far more beneficial, especially for yang dwellings. Dirty water creates shar chi, which brings unlucky vibrations that result in ill health for residents. It is worse if water smells of decaying materials or is muddy. If the drain outside your house stinks, you must do something to clean the drain immediately. Otherwise misfortune will strike in some form.

011 Avoid living on hilltops

If you are in a position to choose where you live, avoid the highest points such as hilltops and penthouses that are located in apartment blocks built on top of a hill. When you are at the highest point, you are not protected from the winds and other elements. In other words, you are vulnerable and will easily succumb to defeat should you find yourself in a competitive situation. You must not think that living on the highest point makes you invincible and strong. On the contrary, it exposes you to attack—the tall poppy syndrome.

012 | Avoid living in a cul de sac

It is also not a good idea to live in an apartment block or a house that is located at the end of a cul de sac. This suggests a situation where, should you get into trouble, there is no way out. Should you find that your house is indeed located at the end of a dead-end road and you do not want to move out, then the way to deal with the situation is to build an inner courtyard with a wall directly facing the road. On the wall place a "window." This enables you to symbolically capture whatever bad chi is being directed at the house. The tranquil serenity of the courtyard transforms any bad chi that enters through the window. Needless to say, the courtyard must be landscaped with healthy growing plants, water features, and good earth energy such as stones or pebbles.

013 Do not face a three-way intersection

This is one of the most widely known afflictions in landscape feng shui. In fact almost all Chinese are so familiar with this particular feng shui taboo that it is difficult for anyone to sell a house that faces an oncoming road to a Chinese family. The oncoming road is regarded as a poison arrow and the best way to solve this problem, should you need to, is to literally block the offending road from view. If your house faces an oncoming road but you are located higher than the road, then the road will not harm you. But if your house is lower than the road, then the oncoming road takes on the hostile energies of a deadly Tiger.

014 Do not live between taller hostile buildings

If yours is an abode hemmed in by two larger buildings, it can cause you to get bullied by your peers and overlooked by your superiors. The remedy for this is to keep the front part of your house well lit. A massive display of yang energy is excellent.

015 | Beware of man-made structures

In addition to natural structures found in the environment, it is also advisable to be mindful of man-made structures that overwhelm your home, thus bringing killing chi into your home. These include transmission towers, hostile looking buildings, sharp edges of buildings, elevated roads, and so forth. Man-made structures are often difficult to counter, so it is best to avoid them completely.

016 Buy regular-shaped property

This applies equally to land and buildings. The basis for building a good feng shui house is a regular-shaped piece of land. Such properties have no missing corners and it is also easier to apply compass formulas more effectively.

017 Use a compass

Even if you are practicing landscape form feng shui, which does not require the compass, it is nevertheless important to get your orientations correct, and for this, you will need a compass. When you use compass feng shui, you definitely require a proper compass. The western style modern compass, which shows the magnetic north, is suitable for feng shui use because this is the north that applies to all compass formulas for yang dwellings.

Directions do not exist in a vacuum; they need a starting point of reference, so stand in the middle of a room to find the Southwest corner of that room; and stand in the middle of the house to locate the Southwest corner of the whole house. Both corners can be activated with good results.

018 | Embrace slow-moving water

The presence of a slow-moving river or stream in front of your home indicates good feng shui. The best is to be "embraced by water." To practitioners of landscape feng shui, when water chi wraps around the house, it creates prosperity vibes to all who live within.

019 Auspicious flow of water

The flow of water is auspicious when it flows past the main door as follows:

- When your main door faces a primary direction, i.e. it faces North, South, East, or West, the water should flow past the main door from left to right.
- When your main door faces a secondary direction, i.e. it faces Northwest, Southwest, Northeast, or Southeast, the water should flow past the main door from right to left.

020 When buying or renting property

Taoists advise that there are some useful omens one can observe when looking at properties to buy or rent. Firstly, it is always best to look at potential property during the early morning hours. The best time would be during the hours of the Dragon between 7:am and 9:am. You can also view property at the hours that correspond to your own animal sign. Secondly, look at the weather conditions—if it rains, it is a good sign, indicating there will be growth luck. If the rain develops into a heavy downpour however, it is not a good sign, because it suggests increasing problems.

021 Use a boy to help you

Old feng shui masters say that the chi energy of a young child, particularly a young male child, is especially accurate when assessing the chi energy of a new property. So it is a good idea to bring a child along when viewing property. The purity of the child's chi energy is such that if the place is not auspicious, it will cause the child to become fretful.

If the child starts to cry or to exhibit signs of distress, the place does not have good chi. If the child starts to pee or becomes difficult, it suggests obstacles. But if the child shows signs of joy, starts to smile and laugh, the omens are good. Trust these signs as they are usually an accurate assessment of the invisible chi energy of the place.

022

Overcome poison arrows with element cures

The element cure depends on the direction the poison arrow is coming from. Thus:

• If the poison arrow is coming from the South, place a large urn of water in front of your door.

• If the poison arrow is coming from the North, place three large rocks or mounds of earth at the front of your house. Hanging a faceted crystal in front of your door is also a good cure.

• If the poison arrow is coming from the West or Northwest, install a very bright light in front of your house. You can also use the color red to simulate fire energy.

• If the poison arrow is coming from the East or Southeast, hang a five-rod metal wind chime in front of your house. You can also use other brass objects such as Fu dogs, coins, or brass rulers.

• If the poison arrow is coming from the Northeast or Southwest, plant trees or incorporate the color green in front of your house. You can also use the color green to simulate the wood energy necessary to overcome the earth energy being sent by the poison arrow.

023 Beware of pointed roof lines

These are deemed to be poison arrows aimed directly at your front door, and at your house. Such physical manifestations of afflictions must be taken seriously because they can cause havoc in your family and business life. If there is a triangular roof line pointed directly at your house coming from the neighbor across from you, try to block it from view or hang a small round mirror to reflect it back.

The traditional method was to hang a Pa Kua mirror, but this will only hurt your neighbor and start an unnecessary feng shui war. A better way to overcome poison arrows such as a triangular roof line without hurting your neighbor is to use the element cure method.

024 How to select a good feng shui house

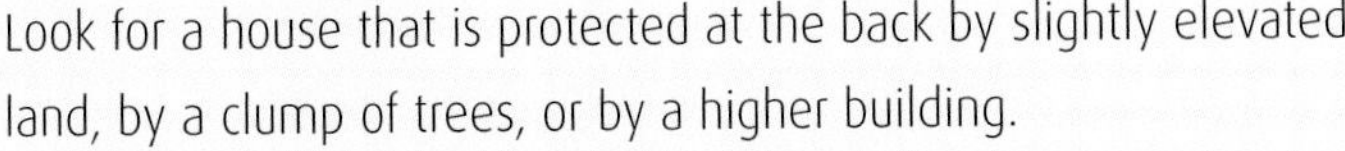

Look for a house that is protected at the back by slightly elevated land, by a clump of trees, or by a higher building.

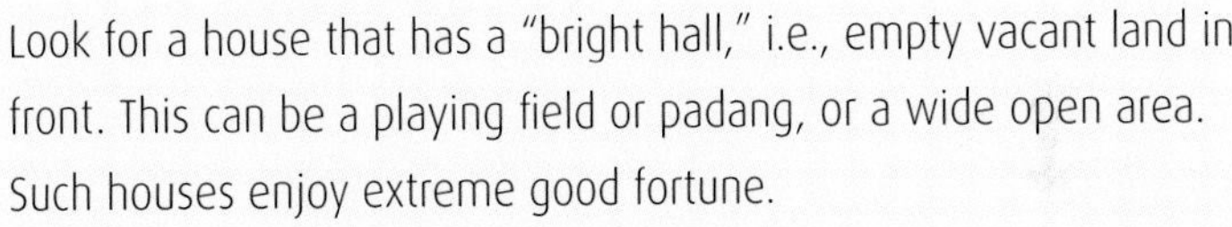

Look for a house that has a "bright hall," i.e., empty vacant land in front. This can be a playing field or padang, or a wide open area. Such houses enjoy extreme good fortune.

Look for a house that has a number that corresponds to your KUA number (*see tip 107*) or to your day of birth. So if you are born on June 18, look for a house with the number 18. If you are born on September 14, then choose a house with number 14. Match it with the day of birth (not the month or year).

Look for a house that is regular in shape with few or no missing corners.

025 Best colors for houses and buildings

Houses and buildings should be color coordinated according to their element. This is based on the house's sitting direction. For example, when the house faces North, it is sitting South.

Buildings that face North are auspicious when they are predominantly red or green. Buildings that face South are auspicious when they are predominantly white or blue.

Buildings that face East and Southwest are auspicious when they are predominantly white or yellow.

Buildings that face West or Northwest are auspicious when they are predominantly green or blue.

Buildings that face Southwest or Northeast are auspicious when they are predominantly yellow or red.

026 House colors to avoid

Houses that face North must avoid being predominantly yellow or blue.

Houses that face South must avoid being predominantly green or yellow.

Houses that face East and Southeast must avoid being predominantly red or blue.

Houses that face West or Northwest must avoid being predominantly white or red.

Houses that face Southwest or Northeast must avoid being predominantly white or green.

027 Regular-shaped houses are best

Avoid living in or building houses that are irregular in shape because this causes imbalances due to missing corners. L-shaped houses can be potentially dangerous if the auspicious corners of the house are "missing." U-shaped houses cause strife and discord between the spouses and such homes suffer from unhappy marriages caused by non-stop quarreling. Irregular shapes caused by extensions to the main house or extra rooms that jut out of certain corners are also generally not a good idea.

It is best to keep houses either square or rectangular in shape. This also makes it easier for residents to benefit from the application of powerful compass formula feng shui.

028 Siting the house auspiciously

Plan the siting of the house carefully. Do not place the house too far in front, nor too far behind when "positioning" it onto a plot of land. Ideally site the house in a way that allows balanced dimensions to be maintained, while at the same time creating the effect of a bright hall in front of the main door. The bright hall can be a garden or a small foyer-like area in front of the main door. When the bright hall is completely missing, chi energy cannot accumulate and wealth luck becomes squeezed.

029 Houses must have yin yang balance

Your house should be designed to receive adequate sunshine and light. When houses are too dark, negative yin energy tends to build up with bad results. At night, lighting should also be adequate. At all times, the yin and yang energy must be well maintained. This means it is not a good idea to allow light to get excessively bright. So at all times, be aware of the need for this vital balance.

030 Driveways should be friendly

Good feng shui is brought into the home when the driveway is non-threatening. This means that there should not be a long driveway pointing straight at the front door of the house. This seems to be so popular with many country mansions in the West and it often brings disastrous results to the family. Instead, driveways should either be placed by the side of the house, or they should be gently curving. Never allow the driveway to become transformed into a poison arrow.

Driveways should also not "narrow" out or in, because this has a limiting effect on the business and finance luck of residents. Lights placed along the driveway create good feng shui for careers.

031 Main doors should be solid and authoritative

The main door of the house should always be solid and authoritative. It should be the largest door in the house and ideally it should face the direction that the house faces. If this is not possible, it is not a big negative. But residents must be aware that there is a difference between the facing direction of the main door and the facing direction of the house. If the main door is not auspicious for any resident of the house, they should use a side door to enter the house. Generally, the main door should be auspicious for the main breadwinner of the house. The auspiciousness of door directions is based on the KUA numbers of individuals and this is founded upon the Eight Mansions formula.

032 Auspicious features of a main door

Main doors should never open inside onto a toilet, a staircase, a solid wall, or a cramped space. These are said to create blockages for the household residents, causing their luck to get conscripted and squeezed. The best option is for the main door to open into a bright hall. In the old days, large family mansions would place an auspicious screen to face the main door, welcoming in the good chi. An auspicious screen causes the energy to flow around the screen into the living room, which is also the bright hall of the home. If you do place a screen in front of the door, make sure it does not tower over the door.

033 Auspicious colors for main doors

Main doors that face South should be painted red.

Main doors that face North should be painted blue.

Main doors that face East or Southeast should be painted green.

Main doors that face West or Northwest should be painted white.

Main doors facing Southwest or Northeast should be painted yellow.

034 When the main door faces an ambivalent staircase

While it is not a good thing for the main door to open onto a staircase, the negative impact worsens when there are two staircases, making the situation ambivalent. It is also bad if there is one staircase going up and another going down, i.e., going up to the higher floors and one down to the basement. This connotes indecision and uncertainty, so that people living in the home will usually suffer from indecision. The best cure for a staircase facing the main door is to hang a well-lit chandelier between them. The presence of bright lights serves to dissolve the uncertain energy.

035 Toilets directly above the main door

This is a major affliction that is more common than expected. There are many apartments that have this nasty problem. The ideal solution is to simply stop using the toilet upstairs. This is of course easier said than done since there are probably only a limited number of toilets in the home. The second best solution is to shine a bright light upwards in the hope of lifting the chi energy surrounding the front door.

036 When the main door is hit by poison arrows

The main door must always be protected from secret poison arrows. This is one of the most important warnings in feng shui practice. Even if the rest of the house enjoys excellent feng shui, when a powerfully strong poison arrow hits your main door, it can negate everything. This rule takes precedence over everything—i.e., they are more important than even the powerful compass formulas and direction-based feng shui.

Poison arrows that can be a potential danger to your front door are anything sharp, pointed, or straight. When directed at your main door, they send lethal energy that cause a string of misfortunes including illness, failure, obstacles, difficulties, and quarrels. They can cause you to lose money, your good name, and just about anything else you hold dear. Secret poison arrows are something to be very mindful about.

One safe way to protect the main door and hence protect the house is to block the offending poison arrow from view. But the best way to repel poison arrows and other negative energy is to place a pair of Fu dogs flanking the main door. Alternatively, opt for wild animals such as Lions or Tigers to "guard" your front door.

037 Examples of poison arrows

A single tree facing your front door can cause havoc in your family life, cause you not to have children, and generally block any good luck from entering your house. If the tree is dead and rotting, it is even worse and you should really try and get it chopped down. If you have to live with the tree, either move your main door's location or place a bright light and paint your door a bright red to overcome this particular poison arrow. Note that if there are several trees facing your front door, they do not constitute poison arrows.

A triangular roof line facing your front door brings severe bad luck, causing illness and creating problems at work and obstacles to your business. The best solution is to block it from view, but if you cannot, then hang five or six rod metal wind chimes between the front door and the roof line.

Other poison arrows are the edge of an overpass, an image of a cross, or a fierce structure across the road. The strength of the hostile energy emitted by these structures depends on how large they are. Usually their effects can be severe and it is best to block them from view.

038 Your main door should not face religious buildings, etc.

The main door should never directly face churches, temples, monasteries, hospitals, prisons, or other places where masses of yin energy build up. When your main door faces such concentrations of yin energy, a very major imbalance gets created and the only way to counter it (if you cannot move) is to paint your main door red. This dash of powerful yang energy will blend with the yin energy to rebalance the forces, causing negatives to be overcome.

Note that it is all right if the religious buildings are at the back of the house or by the side. If this is the case, it is a good idea to paint the wall that faces them red.

039 Your main door should not face a forked road

Your main door should not face directly onto a Y-shaped forked road or path because this symbolizes misfortune and the need to keep on making difficult decisions. It also brings divisions into the family, causing strife among siblings and between spouses. Change the location of the main door if this is your problem.

040 Your main door should not face a mountain

Your main door should never directly face a mountain or hillside, especially if the hillside is less than twenty feet away. When the hillside is too close to the main door, the negative energy becomes even more severe. The result of this affliction includes financial loss, business downturn, and work difficulties. The best solution is to reorient the door to face another direction so that you "capture" the mountain as your back support. By doing this, you will be transforming something harmful into valuable support for your house.

041 Your main door should not face a bend in the road

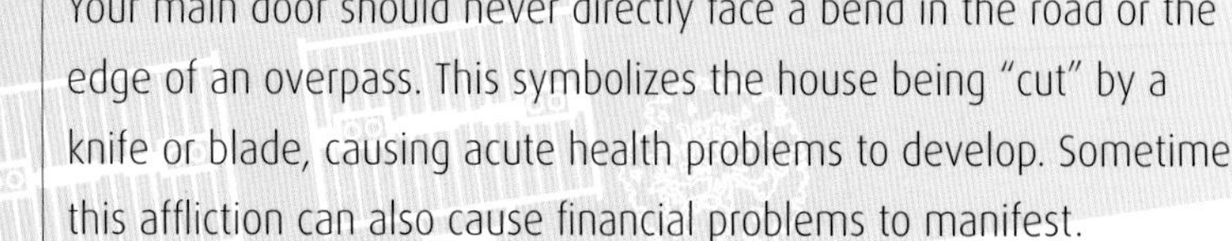

Your main door should never directly face a bend in the road or the edge of an overpass. This symbolizes the house being "cut" by a knife or blade, causing acute health problems to develop. Sometimes this affliction can also cause financial problems to manifest.

042 Your main door should not face a narrow gap between two buildings

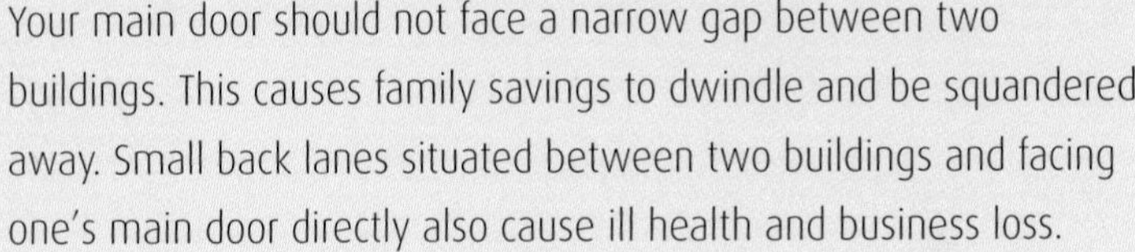

Your main door should not face a narrow gap between two buildings. This causes family savings to dwindle and be squandered away. Small back lanes situated between two buildings and facing one's main door directly also cause ill health and business loss.

043 Your main door should not face a garbage dump

Your main door should not have a large garbage heap in front of it. This causes severe misfortunes and financial loss. If you have your garbage can directly in front of your main door, it signifies loss to your career aspirations and business goals. Better to place garbage bags hidden away, and definitely far away from the main door.

044 Clogged drains must be attended to

If the drains around your house get clogged up with dry leaves and other garbage, you must get rid of the debris as soon as possible. When drains around the home get clogged up, they create blockages in our lives—so projects get stymied and even the flow of chi within the body gets choked up, causing illness to surface. Clogged drains are one of the most severe feng shui problems.

045 | Designing a house layout

Houses with auspicious layout plans create excellent feng shui for the different members of the household. There are different feng shui methods for allocating the different corners of the house to different members of the family. Such allocation can be designed according to the Pa Kua, according to one's astrological animal sign, or according to one of the compass formula methods.

The first step to designing layout is to identify the different sectors of the house based on compass directions. Usually, a house can be divided into nine different sectors with the eight direction sectors plus a central sector. This follows the Lo Shu grid. Thus, each of the sectors signify one of the compass directions.

You must use a compass to demarcate these sectors. If possible, stand in the center of the house to get your orientations. If you cannot, then use your floor plan to mark out the different sectors of the house. Once this is done, you will find it easier to begin allocating sectors to the different members of the family. Always reserve the auspicious sectors for the breadwinner. Other auspicious rooms should be reserved for the dining room and the family room that is used the most, perhaps the TV room.

046 Using the Pa Kua method for house layout

The Pa Kua method requires you to place the father (or patriarch) in the Northwest corner of the house and the mother in the Southwest. The mother can also stay in the Northwest should she choose to do so. The eldest son should sleep in the East of the house, while the eldest daughter should be in the Southeast. This is the easiest method of selecting sectors to place different rooms in the house. The Pa Kua used in this book is based on the later heaven arrangement of the trigrams, which places the trigram Chien (which stands for the patriarch) in the Northwest. Hence under this method, the Northwest is a very important direction. It is a sector that should not be missing from the house.

047 Using astrology in house layout

This is an excellent method for demarcating house layout. Superimpose the astrology wheel over the floor plan of the whole house to determine the sectors best suited to each member of the family. You can also superimpose the wheel inside a bedroom to determine the best sleeping corners for each resident.

You will see that the Rat is placed North, the Horse in the South, the Rabbit in the East, and the Rooster in the West. The other animals are placed in the secondary directions. If you are a Rooster, you should sleep in a room placed West, and if you are a Rat you should be in a room placed North.

048 Using the Eight Mansions method in house layout

A third method of laying out your home is by using the auspicious and inauspicious directions of each member of the family based on their date of birth and KUA number. According to the Eight Mansions formula, everyone is either an East group person or a West group person.

Based on this compass formula, West group people should sleep in one of the four West locations of the home. These are West, Southwest, Northwest, and Northeast.

East group people should sleep in the East group locations of the house. The East locations are the East, North, South, and Southeast sectors of the house.

To find out whether you are an East or a West group person you will need to know your KUA number (*see tip 107*). This is based on your date of birth.

049 Using the Flying Star method in house layout

Another very powerful method of allocating rooms in the house and incorporating them into design layout is using the Flying Star method of feng shui. This is a very potent method that addresses the time dimension of feng shui. Flying Star feng shui enables us to keep updated on the changing energies that occur over time. This method requires one to know how to read the natal charts of houses. These charts show the auspicious sectors of the house, accurately identifying the sectors most suitable for wealth luck, for relationships luck, for health luck, and so on. This method of feng shui also enables one to keep up to date on the changing annual and monthly energies.

The best way to go about designing house layout therefore is to be familiar with the different methods and then to try to incorporate all of the different methods into a balanced feng shui design.

050 Feng shui of doors

Doors are important conduits of energy in the home. There should not be too many doors in the house, since every door signifies a "mouth," and when there are too many mouths in any house, it can lead to quarrels and misunderstandings. Here are a few door taboos that should be observed:

• There should not be three doors in a row, especially if one is the front and the other is a back door, with one door in between. This is an inauspicious affliction. Hang a crystal above the middle door or better yet, place some kind of divider to divert the flow of chi.

• When two doors directly face each other, make sure they are the same width and height. They should face each other directly, although doing so causes a confrontational situation. But this is better than if they only partly face each other, which causes loss.

• When two doors are at a right angle to each other, it is important to ensure that they open and shut into the rooms concerned.

• Two main doors side by side facing the same direction cause the mother and father to be at loggerheads with each other constantly. If you wish to have two doors, one each for the mother and father, then let the doors face different directions.

051 Avoid exposed overhead beams

Never sit under exposed overhead beams, especially if they are structural heavy beams. Sitting or sleeping under such exposed beams causes stress, tension, and headaches to build up. If there are such beams in your house, you can either cover them with a false ceiling, or if this is not a feasible alternative, hang two flutes tied with red thread and place them in the shape of an A on the beam itself. This reduces the killing energy being sent out. Note that if you live in a log house where heavy ceiling beams are part of the style, then the beams are not so harmful. The most harmful are single exposed beams that stand out.

052 Watch out for columns

Feng shui practitioners warn against having stand-alone columns in the home, especially if these are square with sharp edges. The edges cause problems because they send out killing energy. Columns are almost always a feature of large rooms when the building has been done to a budget. So note that if you have columns, the four corners give off poison chi. To remedy this, either wrap the columns with mirrors or place plants around the corners to camouflage them.

053 Staircase feng shui

The staircase should not start directly in front of the main door, or end directly in front of an upstairs door. The chi created is excessively strong and becomes harmful. Staircases are best when they curve gently, rather than being straight and steep. Spiral staircases resemble corkscrews and are strongly discouraged—they definitely should not be located at the center of the house, where they become a poison arrow of the most severe kind. Generally, staircases should be wide and gentle with no "holes" in the steps up.

054 Split levels are not encouraged

It is better not to have split levels in a residence. A ground floor that is made up of different levels tends to suggest instability. However, if you are living in a house with different levels, make sure your dining room is located on the higher level. If you live in a house that has been built against a hillside, make sure the bedrooms are on the upper levels and the kitchens are located on the bottom level.

055 Place kitchens in the back

The kitchen should always be located in the back half of the house. When the kitchen is too near the front, it causes an imbalance of elemental energy in the home. According to the YANG Dwelling Classic, the most auspicious location for the kitchen is the East or South corner of the home. The kitchen must never be in the Southwest, because this hurts the mother, or in the Northwest, because this hurts the father of the family. Another reason to avoid having the kitchen in the Northwest is that this signifies "fire at heaven's gate." In fact, both the kitchen and the stove should never be placed in the Northwest of the house or of the room itself.

056 Mirrors as afflictions

When mirrors are placed in the bedroom and reflect the bed directly, they become the source of a feng shui affliction. Mirrors in the bedroom tend to cause a great deal of problems for the couple sleeping inside the bedroom. They cause the marriage to become crowded. The chi created by large mirrors that face the bed is said to be too powerful for a sleeping person. Also, remember that when you sleep, you are vulnerable to hidden forces and energies that could be reflected into your bedroom. So if you have mirrors in your bedroom, I strongly advise you to either dismantle them or cover them up.

057 Mirrors to improve business

Mirrors can be used to amazing benefit if you run a retail business or if you own a restaurant. When mirrors are used to decorate the walls of a retail operation, they generally attract a much larger crowd of customers. This is because the yang chi created by the people who patronize such establishments will attract even more yang energy, so business improves and grows. It is also a good idea to place a mirror to reflect your cash register, because this "doubles" the sales in the store. If the mirror reflects auspicious symbols of good fortune placed next to the cash register, they will become even more auspicious.

058 Mirrors as remedies

Mirrors can be used to camouflage columns by being wrapped around the column. They are also good for fixing missing corners. They can be used to extend walls, thereby balancing incomplete house shapes. As long as the mirror does not reflect a potentially troublesome image, such as the staircase, toilet, or kitchen, the mirror remedy can be used.

059 Mirrors as enhancers

Clever placement and the use of mirrors in houses and stores can create excellent feng shui. A large wall mirror placed on one wall of the dining room and reflecting the food placed on the table is most auspicious because this "doubles" the food on the table. To be beneficial, the mirror should adequately reflect the food, and it should not be placed in a way that "cuts" the head or feet of residents. In other words, the mirror should be sufficiently large.

Mirrors are also excellent for reflecting good luck symbols and beautiful scenery or gardens. When the mirror reflects outside water into the home, the effect is very lucky. This brings wealth into the home.

060 Avoid irregular-shaped rooms

Odd-shaped rooms or rooms with sloping ceilings can be terribly inauspicious. L-shaped rooms, for instance, symbolize a meat cleaver and unless you are occupying (sleeping or working in) the area that represents the handle (i.e., the short part), you could suffer misfortune. L-shaped rooms are considered to be incomplete and when the missing sector or corner represents a lucky corner, you will lose the benefits of having it. It is common for bedrooms with ensuite bathrooms to be L-shaped.

061 Make your rooms regular in shape

Regular-shaped rooms are easier to feng shui than oddly shaped rooms. If your bedroom is an irregular-shaped room, use furniture and design features to regularize its shape. An irregular bedroom is more important to fix than other irregular-shaped rooms. If the whole house is irregular-shaped, then you can use mirrors to solve the issue of missing corners (as long as the reflection of the mirror does not create another feng shui problem).

062 | Make your toilets inconspicuous

Toilets are best when they are small, inconspicuous, and tucked away into unnoticeable corners. Be wary of locating toilets in the Southwest or Southeast corners of your home. In the Southwest, toilets flush away your relationship luck and could seriously hamper the marriage prospects of eligible residents. In the Southeast, toilets will flush away all wealth-making opportunities. Toilets should also not be located in the middle of the house because this afflicts the heart of the home.

Even when bathrooms are large and luxurious, the toilet itself is best tucked away in a small corner, physically "isolated" from the rest of the bathroom. Do this with a small half wall.

Toilets must also not be located too near the main door because this creates a great deal of bad luck.

063 Furniture placement inside kitchens

It is advisable not to place fire and water elements next to each other or confronting each other. Thus the fridge or dishwasher (both of which signify the water element) should not be placed next to or directly opposite the stove, where heat and fire occur each time food is cooked. The sink should also not be next to the fire element or be directly opposite it.

064 Building extensions to the house

If you build extensions to the house, you must consider the effect of such extensions on the overall shape of the home. Certain shape combinations are beneficial, while others are not. Examine the element of the new extension based on where it is located, i.e., the directional sector it occupies. Check that the element represented by the extension is beneficial for the existing building by ensuring that the element of the extension sector produces, or at least does not harm, the element of the main door direction.

- If the extension is located in the South corner, it represents the fire element. If the main door is located in the West, then the fire element of the extension destroys the metal element of the main door. If the main door is located in the Southwest, however, the fire element will produce the earth element of the main door.

- If the extension is in the Southeast, it represents the wood element. If the main door is in the South, it belongs to the fire element. The extension of wood feeds the fire element of the door, so the effect is auspicious.

065 Some tips for office feng shui

If your office entrance door directly faces an escalator, and at the bottom the escalator faces the main entrance, the effect is bad feng shui, because luck flows outward. If your retail store is facing an escalator in this way, it is also inauspicious.

When the entrance into the office directly faces a row of elevators, the effect is inauspicious. It is like a tiger leaping out at your entrance. The entrance into an office should always be off the elevator lobby.

Do not locate your office entrance door at the end of a long corridor, because this sends killing chi toward the door.

If your office entrance faces another office across the corridor, the effect tends to be confrontational. If it cannot be helped, make sure the doors are perfectly aligned to each other to reduce misunderstandings with the office opposite.

066 More office feng shui tips

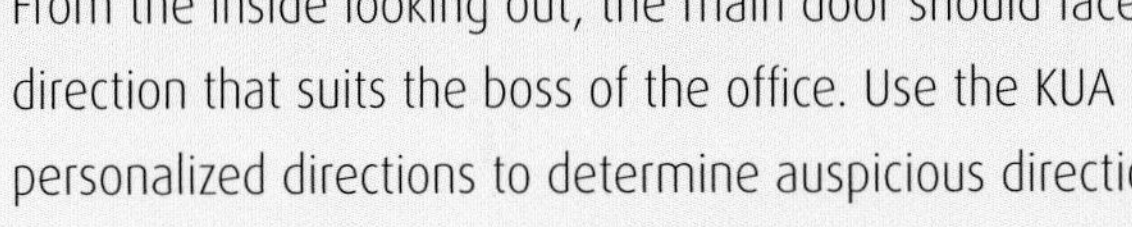

From the inside looking out, the main door should face a direction that suits the boss of the office. Use the KUA formula of personalized directions to determine auspicious directions.

Foyer areas of offices should not be cramped or blocked with boxes or old newspapers. Use mirrors to enlarge the feeling of space, but mirrors should never be directly facing and reflecting the door, otherwise luck simply seeps out.

Make certain the foyer is well lit, even at night, because this increases the store of yang energy, which is good for the office.

If there is a receptionist stationed at the foyer, it is best that he or she does not directly face the door. It is also a good idea to have a wall divider in the foyer area to block the inside office from immediate view.

067 Examples of inauspicious buildings

The luck of most buildings is affected by their location relative to surrounding structures. Here are four examples of inauspiciously located buildings:

- An unlucky configuration caused by a new freeway overpass blocking the main doors.
- A building that is smaller and lower than surrounding buildings: it will be "overwhelmed."
- A building "hit" by a sharp, pointed edge opposite.
- A building located at the end of a dead-end street or a three-way intersection.

068 | More examples of harmful locations

Unlucky configurations are caused by hostile cutting roads and flyovers.

• Buildings can be "hit" by the sharp edges of various neighboring buildings.

• Buildings at crossroads are seldom lucky. Note that corners of buildings also affect each other negatively.

• Buildings can be affected by tall towers directly hitting their main entrances.

069 Place a sailing ship in the foyer

If you place a sailing ship symbol in the foyer, it will bring wealth into the office, but the ship should sail in and not out of the office. The ship should also be filled with ingots and money, because this signifies good fortune. Even better, have the ship sailing from one of the auspicious directions belonging to the boss of the company.

070 Ensure your ship is filled with treasures

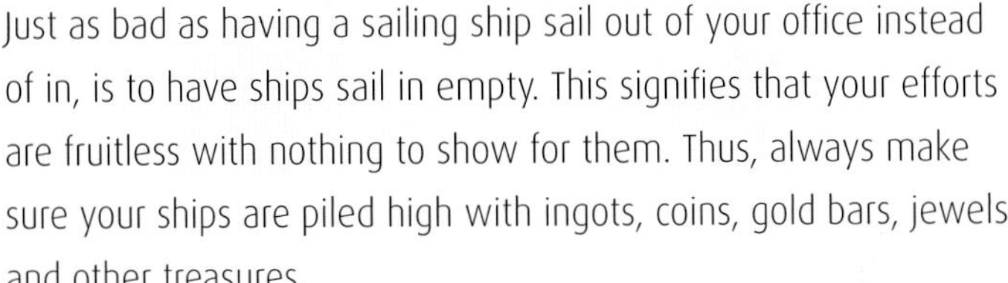

Just as bad as having a sailing ship sail out of your office instead of in, is to have ships sail in empty. This signifies that your efforts are fruitless with nothing to show for them. Thus, always make sure your ships are piled high with ingots, coins, gold bars, jewels, and other treasures.

071 Tips on office arrangements

Long corridors should be avoided. Walkways within any office space should be winding because this slows down the flow of chi. Plants make excellent natural dividers of space. At all costs, avoid having too many dividers, because this creates a cramped feeling. Offices should be well lit and any ventilation system should be frequently cleaned, so air never stagnates.

072 Protruding corners

These are generally regarded as inauspicious structures. They can be compared to sharp knives or hostile fingers pointing directly at the person they hit. The sharp edges may also be pointing directly at the filing cabinets containing important documents, or be facing the door into the manager's office. There are several ways to "dissolve" the bad energy emanating from these poison arrows:

- Plants make very effective foils for protruding corners, but if plants wilt and die after a few months, change them.
- Install a mirror and wrap it around the protruding corner.
- Hang a crystal ball to diffuse the edge of the corner.

073 Managers' rooms

The more senior you are on your floor, the deeper into the office your room should be. The best room is the one in the corner that is diagonal to the entrance door. This is said to be the "wealth" spot of any space. The rooms of big corporate chiefs should follow some feng shui guidelines:

• Regular-shaped rooms are a must. L-shaped and triangular rooms are to be avoided at all costs.

• Projecting corners should be blocked with plants or furniture.

• There should not be any exposed bookshelves, because these are like knives cutting into you.

• If there is a view of the edge of a building from your window, block the view with curtains.

074 Correct desk placement

When your desk is placed in an auspicious position, you will enjoy good fortune at work. Here are some tips:

• Never sit with an open window behind you, because this suggests a lack of support. If the window is closed, it is OK. Always have a wall behind you, and even better hang a painting of a mountain behind you. This gives you solid backing.

• Always sit with the door in front of you. The angle does not matter as long as you sit facing one of your good directions.

075 Some bad desk placements

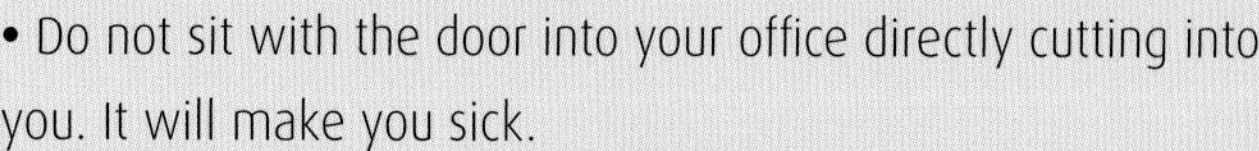

• Do not sit with the door into your office directly cutting into you. It will make you sick.

• Do not sit with your back exposed to the door. You could get "stabbed" in the back.

• Do not sit directly facing another person because this is confrontational, and leads to hostility.

• Do not sit too close to another colleague. Chi quality can get exhausted.

076 Never sit with your back to the door

You should endeavor never to sit with your back to the door. Doing so will cause you to be betrayed by your colleagues or subordinates in the office. There should also not be anything blocking the pathway in and out of your room at work. These signify "obstacles" in your work. If you notice anything harmful hitting your office door, do remove it, or if you cannot, then block it from view.

077 Desk location at work

The best placement for an office desk is somewhere in the middle of the room, with you sitting facing one of your auspicious directions and also facing the door. By your side you can have a window, but a window behind is often harmful unless there is a taller building behind you giving you support. If that building is a bank, it is even better, because this symbolizes having a bank behind you—very auspicious indeed, especially if you are a businessman. A desk placed at the corner diagonal to the entrance door is also lucky.

078 Arranging irregular-shaped offices

If you have no choice and have been asked to occupy an irregular-shaped room, you can introduce some feng shui elements and cures that will make the irregular shape less harmful. Here, the use of lighting can be an excellent way of regularizing the energy of the office. Place some extra lights at the corner of any L-shaped room.

079 Corporate boardrooms

These should be designed to let the big boss sit furthest away from the entrance. There should be a solid wall behind him or her and windows should be by the side of the table. The most important thing to ensure is that all directors attending any meetings should be seated to face their personal best direction according to their KUA numbers. This ensures the best performance from the directors.

080 Allocating rooms to key officers

Based on the Pa Kua Eight Aspirations school of feng shui, the money man or chief financial officer should sit in the Southeast corner, because this is the sector that symbolizes the flow of money. Cash flows will be healthy if the finance chief sits here. Human resource managers should always be placed in the East sector of an office because here good cooperation between staff can be fostered. Research staff should be seated in the Northeast corners, while young trainees are best seated in the North or West. These are, however, general guidelines. For the feng shui enthusiast who knows the more advanced formulas, such as Flying Star feng shui, they should also apply those formulas.

081 Doors inside offices

The main door of any office must be properly designed—solid, large, and always opening into an auspicious space. Main doors must never open directly to a window, staircase, or toilet. These can cause unlucky results for the company. Chi must be able to flow into the office and then gently move deeper into the office. Anything that causes the chi to fly out the window is bad. This rule applies equally to the back of the office. If there are interconnecting doors, these should cause the chi to "meander" rather than flow in a straight line.

- The door into an office must not face a toilet.
- The door should not face a window, or worse, the back door.
- Doors inside the office must never be placed in a straight line.
- Doors in an office should cause chi to "meander."

082 Feng shui of the general office

Furniture inside offices should be symmetrical and well-balanced. Avoid arrangements that cause sharp angles to be formed, such as an L-shaped or U-shaped desk. Avoid having staff sit directly facing each other, because this is confrontational.

Favorable desks and table arrangements affect office productivity by enhancing goodwill and cooperation among the staff. Offices with good feng shui rarely have problems of absenteeism, sickness, politicking, or quarrels.

L-shaped offices tend to cause frequent illness. U-shaped arrangements cause friction between employees. Diagonally arranged tables and seating arrangements cause friction and discord. The best arrangements are those that allow sufficient space for easy traffic within the office. Columns incorporated into the design must be camouflaged with plants. Mirrors can be used to artificially enhance the feeling of space.

083 Color in the office

Use element analysis to design the color scheme of your office. It is a good idea to avoid stripes, crosses, and diamond patterns either on the walls or on the floors. These harbor secret poison arrows that hurt you without you realizing. Allow the color of walls to blend seamlessly from one wall to the next. When in doubt, use neutral colors such as the off-whites and the pastels—and use a single element color to highlight a particular wall or corner that is important or has "good" stars. The area near the door is always important, so painting this in a color to enhance the sitting element is a good idea. Thus, if the foyer area is in the North, white is excellent because white represents metal-producing water—the element of North.

Likewise, use green in the South, use red in the Northeast or Southwest, use yellow in the Northwest or West, use blue in the East and Southeast.

084 Tips on selecting a condominium

Examine the surroundings around the building. Select one that has a clear entrance and a good foyer area where chi can settle and accumulate before entering the building. Look at the approach road leading to the building. Driveways should curve rather than be straight, and the presence of water in front of the entrance is an auspicious feature. The best buildings are usually located on undulating land, being placed neither too near the base of a mountain deep in the valley, nor too high up on hilltops. The best condos are on midlevels.

• Condos built on hilltops lack support and are also not protected from the winds and elements.

• A "mansion" in the sky (i.e., a penthouse built above a building) suffers from the same feng shui affliction.

085 Doors into apartments

The door into the apartment block is far more important than the door entering into the apartment unit itself. Those of you who practice Flying Star feng shui will know that it is the "facing" direction of the building that determines the luck of the apartment unit—at least for the first nine floors. Anything above that needs to be assessed separately. Usually, high-rises have large picture windows that face the city or beautiful scenery. It is this picture window that determines the facing direction of the apartment unit and thus its Flying Star feng shui, when assessing units above the ninth floor.

086 Buildings located on a ridge

Such locations are deemed to be extremely dangerous and inauspicious. There is considered to be no support whatsoever. The same effect is felt when there are roads on two sides of the building (i.e., front and back). Buildings that have roads at both the bottom and the top, or halfway up the building, are also not good. Residents will experience severe afflictions.

087 Pools near condominiums

Swimming pools are a major feature of condominium complexes and these generally attract good chi vibrations, especially when they seem to "hug" the building and are kidney-shaped or circular-shaped. When swimming pools are landscaped with lush plants, they are more auspicious.

Pools are always luckier when located in accordance with Flying Star feng shui, which identifies the luckiest location for water. In the language of Flying Star feng shui, this is where the "water star 8" of the property is located. Flying Star feng shui offers excellent guidelines for the placement of ponds, pools, and other water features to bring wealth luck.

088 Tapping the good chi of the river

There are three excellent ways to "capture" the good chi of rivers and other waterways that flow past the house. For any of these three ways to succeed, the river should flow past the main door.

First, determine the flow of the river. If it flows past the house from right to left, then orientate the main door to face a secondary direction (i.e., Southwest, Northeast, Northwest, or Southeast). If the river flows past the main door from left to right, then orient the door to face a primary direction (i.e., North, South, East, or West). If, in ensuring this direction, the door is tilted 45 degrees to the wall, a castle gate effect has been captured and the household enjoys excellent income luck.

Second, use the Flying Star method to bring the auspicious water star 8 to the front. There are many directions that have this feature in a period 8 chart. Check my book *Flying Star Feng Shui For Period 8* to locate a chart that is best suited to your house and has the water star in front.

Third, simply orient your house to face Southwest. This is because from 2004 to 2024, the Southwest direction is said to be the indirect spirit of period 8, which benefits from the presence of water.

089 Assessing the feng shui effect of a nearby river

If there is a river flowing past your house or anywhere near the vicinity of your house or your condominium complex, it will usually bring good fortune. Generally it should be slow-moving, clean, and unpolluted. Fast-flowing, straight rivers are purveyors of harmful chi energy and can be dangerous, especially when the orientation of your house inadvertently creates energy that clashes with the river.

It is always better to have the river flow past the front of the house than the back, and if the river meanders, then the house should be hugged by the river rather than be "hit" by the protruding part of the river.

090 | Selecting an auspicious apartment

Look for apartments whose entrance direction corresponds to one of your four good directions. This refers both to the entrance into your apartment building and to the entrance to your apartment unit. Apartments that are above the ninth floor are regarded as independent of the building, and hence in such apartments the direction of the largest picture window or balcony is also important. This direction is where chi is coming from. As such, this direction should also correspond to one of your good directions. The Flying Star chart that applies to such high-rise apartments above the ninth floor is usually based on the facing direction of the largest picture window or balcony.

091 Afflictions of apartment entrance doors

It is vital to ensure that the main door into the apartment unit you are considering does not suffer from feng shui afflictions that are hard to remedy. For example:

- There should not be a toilet on the floor above, directly on top of the main door.
- There should not be an elevator shaft opening directly opposite the door into the apartment. The chi coming from the elevator is deadly and killing.
- There should not be a pillar directly facing the apartment door.
- There should not be a staircase directly facing the door.
- The door should not be at the end of a long corridor.

092 | Opening into a spacious interior

On entering any apartment (or any house), the immediate area near the door should not be narrow, cramped, or blocked. Ideally, upon opening the main door, one should have a good view of the living room. The larger the area that the eye can see, the better the feng shui energy tends to be. The diagonal corner furthest away from the main door is an auspicious corner. If you have an auspicious feature in that corner—for instance a suitable enhancer such as water if it is North or Southeast, or crystals if it is Southwest or Northeast—then the entrance chi is said to be excellent.

• The main door should not open to face a toilet. The remedy is to relocate the bathroom door.

• The main door should not open to face a narrow cramped corner. The remedy is to keep the space well lit. Mirrors are a solution so long as they do not directly reflect the main door.

• The main door should not open to directly face a window. This causes the chi to fly out instantly. The remedy is to use draped curtains to keep the window closed.

093 Views from the balcony

In apartment living, balconies that face beautiful views are highly prized. It is a good idea to look for apartments that have a view of rivers, cities, or distant mountains. These are areas that have a good supply of yang chi. Facing a big horizon view is also extremely auspicious. The window should always be kept open, because this allows the chi to flow inside.

If, however, the view from the balcony is the balcony of a nearby apartment, it suggests the buildings are too close and the chi energy is cramped. Grille designs could be sending secret poison arrows to you. In such an instance, it is best to "close" the view.

094 Decorative pillars inside apartments

Stand-alone pillars inside apartments can be a source of killing energy. Round pillars tend to be harmless unless the pillar directly faces a door. Square pillars on the other hand can be quite dangerous, since the sharp edge of the pillar creates killing chi.

- Round pillars that frame the entrance into the living room do not harm the front door.

- A square pillar that faces the front door hurts it. It can be "wrapped in mirrors" or a tree can be placed in front of it to soften its fierce impact.

- The edges of square pillars in penthouse apartments hit at residents seated in the dining and living areas, but if they have been wrapped with mirrors, they are acceptable.

095 Dealing with split levels in an apartment

If there are split or multiple levels in an apartment, bedrooms should be at the highest level, and the dining room should be at a level higher than the living room and the kitchen. The living and public areas of the home can be placed at the lowest levels, but they should be larger than the bedrooms in size. Generally, there should not be more than three different levels in one floor area.

096 Placement of study or home office

When the study is located near the main front door, it encourages you to read, study, and work. This is excellent for working people, or in households with school-going children, and if the study also corresponds to the Northeast sector of the home, it will be especially beneficial for the children. Inside the study, desks and chairs can be placed in a way that is conducive to each child facing his or her best direction for studying. Do, however, avoid exposed shelves, which can act like blades sending out killing energy.

097 Living room placement

This is the entertainment and sociable area of the apartment or house and is best placed near the main entrance into the home. This symbolizes the home welcoming the residents each day. The living room area is also the best place to have feng shui symbolic enhancers—thus the larger it is, the better.

If you can afford it, have more than one living room. Let one living area flow seamlessly into another, thereby suggesting depth. This ensures that good feng shui will last a long time. The living room is also an area where chi tends to accumulate and settle and when the area is large and spacious, it encourages residents to spend more time there. If you are familiar with the Eight Mansions KUA formula feng shui of personalized directions, arrange the furniture in a way that enables every resident to sit facing their respective good directions.

098 Mirrors in the living room

When mirrors successfully enlarge the spaciousness of rooms, they bring good chi. Wall mirrors in the living room are therefore excellent feng shui, as long as they do not directly reflect the main door, or reflect toilets, staircases, and other sources of negative chi. Mirrors should never be placed too low or too high, because this causes an imbalance to the chi energy of the home. Let your mirrors be effective space-enlarging features.

099 Flow of chi in apartments

The interior layout of apartments should be conducive to a good flow and accumulation of chi. This occurs when the movement of traffic flow meanders rather than moves in a straight line. Long narrow corridors are generally discouraged. There should also not be too many windows or doors facing each other in a straight line. Dark cramped corners should be brightly lit and room dimensions should balance.

100 Kitchen locations

Generally, kitchens should never be located in the Northwest because this represents "fire at heaven's gate." They should also not be located in the Southwest because this is the "earth gate" and a fire there would be overwhelming. Locating the kitchen in either of these two locations tends also to hurt the father and mother respectively, because these are their directions.

- Kitchens that are near the main door are unfavorable for children.
- Kitchens are best located in the inner half of the apartment out of view of the main door.
- The stove or cooking area is best placed in the corner diagonal to the entrance door of the kitchen.
- Built-in shelves in any kitchen should be closed with doors. Exposed shelves act like cutting blades and these tend to hurt occupants.
- Kitchens should not be located under a toilet in the floor above.
- Sinks should not be placed next to the stove or opposite the stove.

101 Dragon-tortoise brings career advancement

If you want career advancement in the office, place an image of a dragon-tortoise behind you at work. The image need not be too large, but the heavier it is, the better. Something made of brass would be ideal. The dragon-tortoise combines the celestial chi of two powerful creatures—and while the tortoise brings universal protection and support, the dragon protects against brashness and impulsiveness in decision-making. If you wish, you may also wear the image of the dragon-tortoise as an amulet ring. Wear it on your middle finger on your right hand with the head facing outward for maximum effect. This brings beneficial career opportunities.

102 Rooster diffuses office politics

If you feel very intimidated at work, it could be due to unfriendly politicking by envious or ambitious colleagues. A very effective feng shui cure for this is to place a majestic-looking rooster or cockerel in the office. Either will be excellent to devour malicious gossip and ill intentions aimed at you. The Rooster is said to derive its magnificent ability to put a stop to gossiping and backbiting from the red comb above its head, as well as the powerful claws on its feet. There are those who also believe that the Rooster is in reality the celestial phoenix, and thus has the ability to transform into the celestial bird when needed. The Rooster takes on added influence during the years of the Rooster.

103 Is there a poison arrow aimed at you?

It is really important to make sure you do not have anything pointed, sharp, or triangular behind you, pointing directly at your back. For example, the edge of a cupboard or bookshelf. Maybe there is an abstract painting playing havoc with your support system. These are secret poison arrows that harm and hurt you. If you want to ensure good feng shui around your work area, develop awareness for everything that surrounds you. When there is something that has the effect of a secret poison arrow "stabbing" you behind, you will meet up with one misfortune after another.

If you do discover something like this, the remedy is to block it from view or better yet, if you can, remove it completely.

104 Bright colors to counter yin spirit exhaustion

If you find yourself short of energy and constantly overcome by tiredness or lethargy, it is possible that you are suffering from "yin spirit exhaustion"—too much yin. The remedy is to wear some strong yang colors such as reds and yellows, and whites. If you do not counter the effect you could either fall very ill or, worse, you could find yourself surpassed at the office. Yin spirit exhaustion is a fatal feng shui condition that depletes you of energy. To help you back on your feet again, place a powerful Dragon Ru Yi on your left side at work. This will boost your chi levels and have you feeling better immediately.

105 Three coins for prosperity

For those in business, taping three Chinese prosperity coins tied with red or gold thread onto cash registers, invoice files, and even desktop computers creates the footprints for wealth luck to follow. This is said to be an efficient way of increasing business sales and profits. It is also a great idea to keep three coins tied with red string inside your wallet to ensure you always have a good and steady flow of income. This is an effective way to ensure that you never run out of cash.

106 Keep bathroom doors closed

Make it a household habit to keep all doors going into the bathrooms of the home closed at all times. Bathrooms are places where negative energies tend to accumulate and these are best kept locked inside. Do not activate bathrooms with auspicious symbols because they will almost always backfire. For instance, wealth energizers inside the bathroom create "bad money" that will eventually get you into trouble. Love energizers in the bathroom create "afflicted romances," such as romances that bring problems and heartaches.

107 Sit facing your sheng chi direction for good luck

This is the direction that brings you the best kind of material wealth and growth luck. The sheng chi direction is what career-minded people or those in business are most in need of tapping. This is usually regarded as the "best" direction for everyone, based on the powerful Eight Mansions formula.

Everyone's personal KUA number is based on their gender and date of birth. From these personal details, you are able to calculate your KUA number. There are altogether nine KUA numbers and each of these belongs to either the East or West group of directions. To find out your KUA number here is the formula:

• Take the last two digits of your year of birth and add them together until the number is reduced to a single digit. If you are born in January you should adjust for the lunar year and deduct one year from your year of birth before applying the formula.

• Next, if you are male, you deduct the number thus obtained from 10 and the result is your KUA number. If you are female, then you add 5 to the number obtained and the result is your KUA number. (For males born in year 2000 and after, subtract from 9. For females born in year 2000 and after, add 6.)

107

- The result of the second step leaves you with a number that you should once again reduce to a single digit. This is your personal KUA number.

To discover your sheng chi direction, simply check your KUA number against the small chart here:

- If your KUA is 1 your sheng chi is Southeast.
- If your KUA is 2 your sheng chi is Northeast.
- If your KUA is 3 your sheng chi is South.
- If your KUA is 4 your sheng chi is North.
- If your KUA is 5 your sheng chi should be read as 2 for men and 8 for women.
- If your KUA is 6 your sheng chi is West.
- If your KUA is 7 your sheng chi is Northwest.
- If your KUA is 8 your sheng chi is Southwest.
- If your KUA is 9 your sheng chi is East.

Once you know your sheng chi direction, always sit facing it, especially for all your important speaking engagements and telephone conversations. This is one of the most potent feng shui practices. Carry a pocket compass to get your directions right.

108 Using mirror remedies in the office

If you have the misfortune to occupy an irregular-shaped room at work, try using a mirror to regularize the shape. This is one of the most efficient ways of regularizing a room. Using mirrors in the office is a luck-bringing practice, since mirrors are usually able to double your good fortune. What you should also know is that mirrors can also double your misfortune, so the view it reflects and where you place it is what's most important. Always ensure mirrors reflect auspicious images, and never toilets, garbage cans, or silly things like that. Secondly, always ensure there are no affliction "stars" occupying the corner of the room where you plan to hang a mirror on the wall. Affliction stars are related to Flying Star feng shui.

109 Amethysts bring harmony in relationships

Amethysts are powerful crystals for enhancing good health and great relationships. Amethyst chips placed as leaves on gem trees are excellent for enhancing harmony at home and in the office. Placed in the Northeast or Southeast, they smooth out obstacles that impede success. Amethyst geodes in their raw rock state have powerful energy when activated with a red string. Place such a geode under the marital bed and tied to the bed post (bed posts on both sides would be most beneficial) near the bottom part of the bed to ensure marital fidelity between spouses. This is a Taoist ritual for ensuring the husband does not fall prey to predatory females.

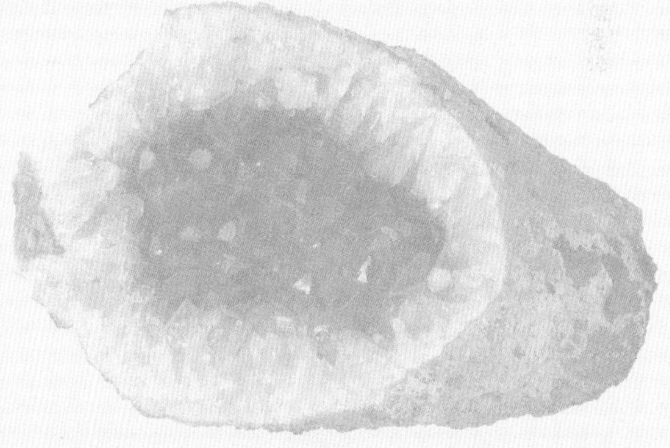

110 Boost your career with good mentor luck

Hang a picture of the company's big boss on the Northwest wall of your office or at the home to create the luck of patronage, and to attract influential friends into your life. This has the powerful effect of creating valuable mentor luck. You will find that your efforts get recognized and find favor with the decision-makers within your company. Mentor luck comes in the form of greater opportunities for advancement within your work environment. For those in business, activating the Northwest attracts powerful influence in the corridors of power, which brings enormous commercial benefits.

111 | Go for high ceilings

High ceilings always create good growth energy. They counter the kind of chi that stunts one's growth. There is of course no need to overdo this, but if you have a choice, create a feeling of space to enable yourself to "grow." Physically, your space should never have a feeling of being stunted. Low ceilings tend to create this feeling.

112 Lights should be in front, not behind

A bright light shining behind you can lead to disloyalty and betrayal. It creates unbalanced energy in your space and lights up the wrong places. Desk lights especially must never be directed to the back. Instead, always keep the front part of your office well lit. Ceiling lights should also be directed to the space in front of the desk—this creates a symbolic bright hall effect, allowing chi to settle and accumulate in front of you. It is only when chi settles gently in front of you that you are able to benefit from it.

113 Work areas must be well lit

Keep your office lobby and desk area at work well lit at all times. It is light that brings the precious yang energy that causes good fortune to accumulate. When office areas are kept dim and poorly lit, dark yin forces will dominate, leading to lethargy and a lack of creativity and work energy. Employees will demonstrate productivity blocks and a general sense of lethargy. For the same reason, you should ensure that all bulbs that are no longer working are changed immediately. Never allow work areas to become dominated by yin energy.

114 | L-shaped desks & facing directions

Unlike L-shaped rooms, L-shaped desks are not a big problem in feng shui, but they are certainly not ideal. The important thing is to ensure the desk is oriented so that you sit facing your sheng chi direction, or one of your four good directions based on the KUA formula. For work or business success, it is always a good idea to capture the sheng chi direction, but if you cannot, then at least make certain you do not sit facing one of your loss directions. Those of you with L-shaped desks should ensure that if you face two directions (because of the computer) both directions are favorable.

115 | Arowana fish for business luck

Chinese businessmen are fond of keeping a golden arowana (or dragon fish) in the North or Southeast corner of the office. They believe this fish attracts business growth and profit expansion. If you plan on following this tip, you will not need more than a single fish. Arowanas never get lonely and they thrive best when kept alone. Do not feed your arowana with live bait because this creates bad karma and any profits you make might be tainted. Instead, train your arowana to accept food pellets. Always ensure the fish tank is clean and properly aerated. A happy fish is what will bring good fortune. This is because happy fish create "happy water," which in turn attracts good fortune.

116 Carp & goldfish bring abundance

Other good feng shui fish are goldfish and carp—especially those with vibrant red colors. These can be kept in ponds (at least 33 inches deep) or in aquariums. When fish are kept for feng shui reasons, they must be placed in the correct sectors of the living or dining rooms or in the correct corners of the gardens. The water should also be clean and well oxygenated so that the fish are free from disease. Nothing brings greater abundance than happy fish. When they are lethargic or diseased, it is always due to poor water quality and this will affect the chi energy of the home. One of the best-kept secrets of the Taoists is that poor water quality causes unbalanced chi to emanate into the environment around the water. If you allow the water quality in your fish tank to emit unbalanced chi, the water feature does more harm than good. So do make certain your filtration system is efficient. Never keep fish inside the bedroom, in bathrooms, or in the kitchen. These are serious feng shui taboos.

117 Be careful of overhead beams

Ensure there are no exposed beams on the ceiling. These tend to press down on the luck and the physical well being of those below. Where the design of ceilings calls for heavy beams to span the length or breadth of the room, these tend to create a depressive effect on residents. This is a physical feng shui affliction that can get very serious in apartment buildings where the problem is magnified by the multiple levels pressing down, one on top of the other. If there are overhead beams on your ceilings, make a special effort to avoid sitting or sleeping directly under them. Another solution is to hang a pair of hollow bamboo stems or "flutes" on the beams. This helps to dissolve the sharp killing energy that they create.

118 Abstract paintings can cause problems

Abstract paintings often carry secret poison arrows that can create feng shui harm, especially if there are triangles, crosses, and strong lines featured. When the paintings incorporate suggestions of any of the five elements, either through the dominant color of the paintings or the use of dominant shapes, it is a good idea to undertake an element analysis to determine if the painting in question is beneficial or harmful in the corner where it is hung. This requires you to be familiar with the three cycles of relationships between the elements as well as the images and colors representative of each element. Thus circular shapes, which represent metal energy, would be excellent in the West and Northwest; or in the North where metal produces the sector's water element. But circular shapes can be harmful in the East and Southeast. So make this kind of analysis before displaying your latest abstract masterpiece.

119 | Create a "harbor" to attract wealth luck

Sailing ships made of gold and laden with gold ingots, coins, or precious gems are believed to bring excellent business luck. Placing ships in the home or office is a very auspicious thing to do, because it is like creating a "harbor" of ships, where each ship brings one source of income. Many ships mean many sources of income. So, if you have many ships in your office, they indicate a prosperous harbor and every ship signifies a different source of income. For companies, this expands the company's sources of income, thereby boosting profits quite impressively. You must watch out that any ship you display does not have nails or cannons sending secret poison all through the room. Pictures of sailing ships hung in wealth corners like the Southeast or in the CEO's office are said to attract good fortune brought by the winds and waters.

120 | Paintings at work

If your desk at work faces an empty wall, create your own personal "bright hall" effect by hanging a painting or print of a wide-open field or space. Another great idea is to hang a picture of a harvest scene. There are some magnificent oil paintings coming out of Bali that depict the harvesting rituals of the rice farmers there. Such paintings always suggest that one's good fortune is about to "ripen," ready for harvesting. Paintings to avoid are those that depict wild animals—tigers with their mouths open—war scenes, or paintings with social messages. Instead, paintings should always suggest and imply abundance and success. And the office is no place for sensual paintings since these tend to create distraction chi.

121 Avoid love activators in the office

Auspicious symbols of love like the mountain peony are great for the home, but can cause problems at the workplace. Leave these at home. When you activate for love and romance at the office, you run the risk of inadvertently creating situations that lead to scandals and indiscretions. They are also a source of major distraction and will only deplete you of creativity and productivity. So do not place birds in pairs or have the double happiness image near you at the office. These are better placed in the home. Keep work areas activated with success-bringing symbols in the career area.

122 Always be aware of the door location in the office

Don't sit with your back to the door. This can lead to backstabbing. If you are senior enough to enjoy a private room, you should always ensure that you sit with the door visible. Using a mirror to "correct" this is at best only a cure. It does not completely overcome the betrayal chi that is created. It is worse when the door into your office is placed directly behind you, because this suggests killing chi.

When the door is diagonally behind you, the chi is exhausting you. Doors that are placed by your side on the right indicate hostility coming into the office, while doors placed by your side on your left are less harmful. The best arrangement is when the door is diagonally in front of you on your left side. This suggests opportunities and good fortune. If this door also faces your sheng chi direction, the beneficial effect is even greater.

123 Block off bad views

Use curtains to block off inauspicious views, such as garbage dumps or smoky factory chimneys. These tend to emit yin chi that causes you to lose your concentration and your energy. They are not, however, as harmful as views of poison arrows that send out killing chi. These would be the sharp edge of a nearby building, triangular roof lines, or hostile-looking architectural effects. Buildings with glass that directly reflect your building are said to "absorb" all your yang essence. In all these latter examples, you should block off the view with heavy curtains.

124 Long corridors are like arrows

Avoid sitting at the end of a long corridor. This is like a giant poison arrow aimed at you. It is a rule that applies equally to the location of offices. If your office is placed at the end of a long corridor, you will find it difficult to have much success, since harmful energy is being sent toward your door daily. In the home, the room that lies at the end of a narrow corridor suffers from the same affliction. This is something that should be incorporated into house, apartment, and office designs at the planning stage. If you are already located at the end of a long corridor, the remedy is to literally "distract" the fast-moving chi energy. Slow it down by placing paintings along the wall. If the corridor is not too narrow, place water features and plants to generate a winding effect.

125 Confrontational seating causes discord

Confrontational seating arrangements lead to discord and disharmony in the workplace. This is because those sitting opposite each other are said to be "challenging" one another. It is better to have windmill-shaped workstations where each person has his or her own private space and is not directly facing other people. If you cannot change your existing office arrangement, display Rooster images in the office to take away the hostile energy. If you do not cure your office of hostile energy, the air becomes afflicted with a great deal of tension, which in turn produces an air of misery and frustration. Such offices rarely have happy energy. Turnover will be high and you will experience greater levels of absenteeism and sickness among staff.

126 Feng shui your important files

Stick Chinese prosperity coins, good luck calligraphy, and auspicious stickers to important files and logbooks. When your sales book is suitably enhanced, for instance, you will find that your sales will start to increase. Invoice books can be similarly activated for good luck when you place auspicious symbols such as the Dragon or Tortoise or the symbol of the five bats of abundance. There are tiny carved jade symbol bookmarks and cellphone holders and these, together with the three coins tied with red mystical knots, are ideal. In feng shui, good fortune can be "activated" with as many auspicious symbols as you wish and everything that you use at work can be activated—from phones to computers and briefcases to pens. Imbue your symbols of good fortune with positive yang chi by mentally transferring your concentration onto the symbols. Use the power of your own mental consciousness.

127 Lucky logos bring growth and success

Choose a corporate logo that has an auspicious meaning. The Chinese, for instance, love using the image of the dragon, birds, sailing ships, tortoises, fish, and so forth. They rarely (if ever) use abstract designs that have sharp edges pointing at their names on a calling card. For example, never have a logo that seems to be pointing downward, as this suggests downward-moving chi. I draw your attention to the logo of Enron, the American company that has gone bust. Enron's logo is a big E, except that instead of having the E stand straight and tall, the logo has the E tilted so that the letter stands precariously on its edge. Looking at the logo in front of its head office building, one gets the impression it is going to topple over at any moment. No one should have been surprised when this once-powerful company collapsed.

Corporate logos should be in color combinations that do not clash. Use the five element cycles to determine this. For instance, the color red is auspicious when combined with green or yellow, and less so when combined with black or blue. The color black is best when combined with white to form the yin and yang balance. White is also said to be very harmonious with black.

128 Selecting the right colors

Memorize the productive cycle of the five elements, and then use it to enhance good luck. For instance, when considering colors, note that fire is red and produces earth, which is yellow. So red enhances yellow or earth corners.

The productive cycle of the five elements is the key that unlocks the enhancing techniques of feng shui. Thus, when you wish to activate any corner within the home, just note the element of that corner based on its compass direction, and then enhance it with anything or any color that generates the relevant producing element for that corner. For instance, say you wish to activate the Southeast for wealth. Note that this direction is the element wood. To produce wood, you will need water. So anything blue or black or having a water feature will activate this corner.

Earth produces metal, which is gold or white, and this in turn produces water, whose colors are black and blue. Water produces wood, which can be green or brown, and this in turn produces fire, which is red.

129 Boost your confidence with red

Red is the color that is best to wear if you need a boost in confidence. It is excellent if you are in the selling profession. Red is excellent as a source of added energy to close sales. Red is not merely the color of the fire element; it is also suggestive of the strong, assertive person. Red is particularly effective during the winter season when its yang essence will provide an excellent balance to the yin darkness of winter.

130 Blacks and blues generate a calming influence

Wear blacks, blues, and dull colors to calm a hot temper. These are yin colors that are an effective foil against excessive yang energy. These are also colors that signify the water element and thus belong to the North corners of rooms, offices, and homes. Anywhere, in any space where you spend a good deal of your waking hours, you can use a compass to pinpoint the North corner and in that corner place something blue or black—this acknowledges and activates the water element of the corner, bringing a calming influence, while energizing your career luck at the same time.

131 White makes you authoritative

Wear white for increased assertiveness and authority. This is especially effective when combined with a silver or gold brooch or pin. This is in fact the perfect color for career women who want to push aggressively forward in their profession. White also lends strength to those keen on making it to board level—this is because white is not only the perfect yang chi simulator, it also suggests metal element energy, which signifies the power of the Chien trigram. So whenever you have an important meeting, negotiation, or event where you need to put your best foot forward professionally, wear white.

132 Get to know the feng shui ruler

It is a good idea to invest in a feng shui ruler, which reveals all the auspicious and inauspicious dimensions, which you can apply to everything from table heights to calling cards and custom-made furniture. Such rulers are easily available and generally offer four sets of auspicious and four sets of inauspicious dimensions. These are given in centimeters as well as inches. Feng shui dimensions seem to be most effective when used on doors and table heights.

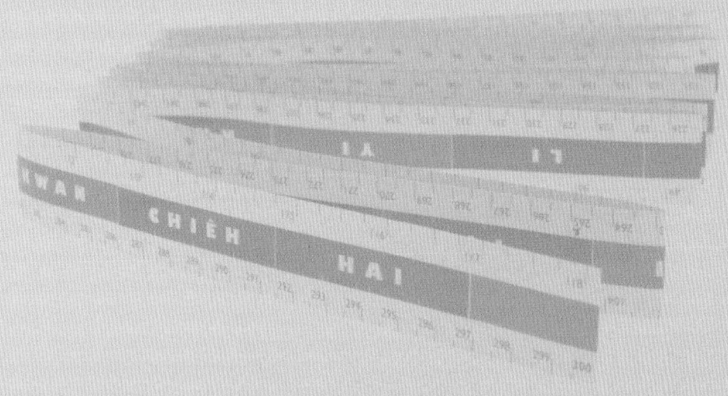

133 Stunted trees have no place in feng shui

Artificially stunted trees (bonsai) are symbolically bad for those in business or embarking on a career. Do not confuse bonsai with artistically pruned trees and plants. In recent years, many companies have perfected the art of pruning and have produced exquisitely shaped shrubs that are excellent feng shui. Bonsai, on the other hand, are trees that have been artificially stunted. These emit the kind of chi that run counter to the natural chi of the wood element and are thus not recommended, especially in the wood element corners of East and Southeast. If you collect bonsai and love the look of these miniature trees, keep them by all means, but keep them out of the wood element corners.

134 Too many plants in the North will exhaust career luck

Avoid having too many plants or wooden objects in the North sector of your office or desk. The wood element exhausts water and tends to hurt the North corner. This has negative implications for your career luck. Use the same reasoning also on fresh flowers. The corners for placing a decorative vase or basket of flowers are in the East and Southeast of rooms and tables. This enhances good health and wealth luck. Remember to throw out flowers after they have faded. Stale water and dying blooms spoil the energy of rooms.

135 Keep an arowana image on your desk

If you cannot keep a real arowana, get an arowana figurine and keep it on your desk. Remember that feng shui is a skill that uses a great deal of symbolism and man-made paintings and images are often as effective as the real thing. It is not a bad idea to have a school of nine arowana displayed artistically in your office, although a single one should be good enough to create wealth luck. The arowana is widely acknowledged as the Dragon in feng shui. Businessmen are very fond of keeping this fish to expand their wealth luck.

136 Avoid "hostile" creatures near you

Do not have pictures of wild animals that look and feel fierce anywhere within view of your desk, especially facing you. They will literally deplete you of energy, and if their mouths are open, they could even "eat you up." It is for this reason that I strenuously advise against displaying paintings of tigers that seem to be on the prowl. They become something dangerous, especially for those born in years of small animal that are not astrological "friends" of the tiger. Even fiercer than the tiger, in effect, is the lion. The Chinese always place the "lion" outside, thereby turning it into a protector guardian. Even then, Taoist masters go to great lengths to warn against indiscriminate use of the lion image. They say the lion is most suitable for large buildings such as palaces, temples, museums, and multi-story buildings, but may be too strong for residential dwellings.

137 Face a good direction when you negotiate

If your work requires you to be frequently involved in high-level negotiations, make sure you carry a small compass and are familiar with your good directions. This enables you to negotiate facing one of your good directions. When you use your personalized auspicious directions, you will be applying one of the most powerful feng shui formulas. Make it a habit to be aware of orientations in the office and your place of work. Chinese feng shui always uses the compass when applying feng shui principles, so you should become familiar with this important tool.

138 Carry a pocket compass

Keep a pocket compass with you at all times so that you can quickly check your orientations. This enables you to practice spontaneous feng shui, and all you will need to know beforehand are your good luck directions. Remember to face your sheng chi direction for success luck and to face your love direction for romance. Carrying a compass also enables you to undertake a quick makeover: moving decorative items in hotel rooms and temporary offices, should there be a need to do so. It is never advisable to try to guess compass directions and locations, because inaccuracy often makes your feng shui practice less effective.

139 Invoke the power of the Dragon

Wear a dragon brooch or tie pin to give you strength, courage, and protection in a dog-eat-dog world. In Chinese culture, the five-clawed dragon is regarded as the most auspicious symbol. The Dragon is the ultimate symbol of good fortune and having a dragon in the house beside a water feature such as a pond or aquarium, and wearing a dragon either as a brooch or a ring, invokes the great power of this celestial creature. The Dragon is said to symbolize the emperor as well as the wealth-bringing cosmic chi. Even if you do not believe in feng shui, it is an excellent idea to have a dragon image in your office and in your home. However, do not keep the dragon in the bedroom and do not have dragon images on your carpets or mats. Stepping on an auspicious creature is never good feng shui.

140 Capture your love direction

Your love direction is known as your nien yen direction, and tapping this sitting direction when out on a date, or pointing your head toward it when sleeping, brings you the luck of love and good relationships. This applies to family, your spouse, your parents, and also your children. The nien yen direction brings you love and also helps you maintain this love and happiness in your life.

Your personal nien yen direction is based on your KUA number.

To discover your nien yen direction, check your KUA number against the information opposite:

140

- If your KUA is 1 your nien yen is South.
- If your KUA is 2 your nien yen is Northwest.
- If your KUA is 3 your nien yen is Southwest.
- If your KUA is 4 your nien yen is East.
- If your KUA is 5 your nien yen is like 2 for men and 8 for women.
- If your KUA is 6 your nien yen is Southwest.
- If your KUA is 7 your nien yen is Northwest.
- If your KUA is 8 your nien yen is West.
- If your KUA is 9 your nien yen is North.

Once you know your nien yen direction, use it to create happiness and love luck.

141 Perfect place for the computer

The Northwest and West corners are the perfect sectors for all your metal machines and tools such as your computer. Computers or other metallic objects activate the luck of patronage, bringing influential people into your life. This tip is based on the eight aspirations of the eight-sided Pa Kua formula and is generally very effective. It is a good idea to undertake an annual update to ensure that these locations are not afflicted during the year by any of the misfortune stars. If either the West or Northwest is afflicted, you might have to move your computers and fax machines to another corner. This is because these "machines" in the office cause chi energy to become activated each time they are used. So when the space they occupy is "afflicted," these machines cause the affliction to manifest as illness, obstacles, quarrels, and accidents at the office.

142 Do not face a mirror at work

Do not sit at your work desk facing a big mirror directly in front of you. This causes all your luck to be dissipated, literally sucked from you by the mirror. According to many Taoist feng shui masters, mirrors tend to "absorb" your spiritual essence when they directly reflect your face or your back, especially when your mind is engaged or concentrated on other matters. These are moments when you tend to be most vulnerable. Mirrors that are hung on walls on either side are less harmful, although it is preferable for there not to be mirrors that are too close to you. They should be at least six feet away. In fact, it is not a good idea to have mirrors in the office at all, since these tend to attract "devils" into the office. If you use mirrors in the general office, it is necessary to keep the office well lit (i.e., the office must be infused with a good dose of yang energy). You should also have plants next to them to ensure that yin energy does not prevail.

143 Music creates yang chi

When the office environment gets too quiet, it is a good idea to allow those working there to enjoy their music. Sound energy is an effective way of activating good energy and also a great way to maintain a good tai chi balance of yin and yang. It is only important to ensure that sounds do not get so loud that they create blocks to creativity and concentration within the office.

144 Beware the Five Yellow

In any year, always take note of where the deadly Five Yellow is, and then avoid sitting or disturbing the sector it occupies. For instance, if this year the Five Yellow flies to the Northwest, it means that this troublesome annual affliction, which brings misfortunes, bad luck, loss, illness, and accidents, affects the Northwest sector of all structures. This includes houses and offices, and its evil effects are usually felt not only in the Northwest of the building, but also in the Northwest of individual rooms and offices.

145 Keeping track of annual afflictions is a vital part of feng shui practice

Keeping track of the annual afflictions is one of the most important dimensions of feng shui practice. In places like Hong Kong and Taiwan, large companies retain feng shui experts on their payroll to ensure that the feng shui of their offices and of their most senior managers is kept up to date each year. Note that the Five Yellow is not the only affliction to beware of. Each year, different sectors are afflicted with different kinds of misfortune and it is necessary to keep track of which sectors of the home or office are afflicted. Only then can you apply the remedies. The remedy for the Five Yellow is either the six-rod all-metal hollow wind chime, or better still, the five-element pagoda made of chrome or brass.

146 Locate the power place at work

The "power place" at the office is always the space that is diagonal to the entrance. If you are placed in this corner, chances are you will eventually emerge as the most important person in the office, the best producer, the most highly respected, or the most authoritative. Those in power at the office should give themselves this spot, because this ensures they will have fewer problems in being obeyed and respected. Managers and supervisors should take note of this if they do not know the more advanced formulas of feng shui. Being diagonal to the entrance deep inside the office brings excellent power feng shui.

147 Symbols of upward mobility

The Chi Lin and the phoenix are other fantastic symbols for upward mobility in one's career. A single Chi Lin—the horse with the dragon head—brings swift success, courage, and supreme confidence, which are the desired attributes of corporate high fliers. Place the Chi Lin either as a painting or as a plaster, clear acrylic, brass, crystal, or ceramic symbol behind you at work. The phoenix brings amazing opportunities for those on the fast track to power and success. Corporate players will discover the incredible benefits of having the phoenix present in their workspace. The benefit is also felt when worn as pins on shirt lapels. Phoenix rings and pendants are so efficient at attracting opportunities that unless you are able to keep up, you could end up having feng shui that is simply too good. Remember that opportunities need to be developed and this requires hard work.

148 The wish-fulfilling cow

Display the wish-fulfilling cow for prosperous harmony in your office. Not many people are aware of the benefits of having the cow image at work. In India, the cow is regarded as a sacred animal. To the Chinese, the cow is associated with the nurturing earth energy, which has the power to fulfil all your dreams of wealth and prosperity. Cows also bring wisdom to households that carry their image. Wish-fulfilling cows are best visualized lying on their sides surrounded by coins and golden ingots. If you are able to find such images, they should be placed in the compass direction of Northeast or they should be facing Northeast.

149 The amazing wealth wallet

Create a wealth wallet to be kept in your work drawer. Tie three Chinese coins together and place in a red packet (ang pow). This is symbolic of you always having money when you need it. A wealth wallet should have many compartments to signify many sources of income and these should be filled with high-denomination money, preferably from several different countries. Wealth wallets should never be empty, but instead should be bulging with money. Wealth wallets should never be made of cheap plastic material. They should be made of leather, silk, or other expensive material. They are extremely auspicious when red or yellow in color. Black wallets are also lucky, as long as there is a red packet kept within.

150 The ringing bell brings customers

Use the ringing bell made from seven metals to attract business to your company, and customers to your retail store or restaurant. This is one of the most effective ways to increase your sales. In the old days, it was believed that the bell was the implement of one of the Dragon sons and that it was always used to attract good fortune. The magic lies in the deep resonant tones emitted when the bell is struck by a wooden mallet, and this can only be achieved when the bell is made from the same seven metals used to create the singing bowl. These seven metals are said to represent the seven planets of the universe, as well as the seven chakras or energy points of the human body.

151 Cleanse office chi regularly

Don't let the chi in the office go stale or become thick with negative energy. This kind of chi can cause illness to manifest and quarrels to occur. It also causes things to go missing, problems to crop up unexpectedly, and projects to get stuck. Nothing hurts business quicker than stale energy in the office. This happens more often than most of us realize because fresh air simply does not have a chance to get into our heated and air-conditioned offices.

In cold countries, where offices are heated, the air inside office buildings also gets hurt because what flows through such offices is usually recycled air. There are some offices that have not enjoyed fresh air for years.

The easiest and best way to cleanse invisible stale chi is by using a singing bowl that is made from the seven metals that represent the seven planets. These metals include silver and gold, which signify the moon and the sun. Strike the singing bowl in a rhythmic way as you walk round the office and inside rooms, paying close attention to corners. At first, the bowl will emit rather flat sounds, but after a while, when the air has been cleared, the sounds of the bowl become purer and more clear.

152 A bank behind you ensures financial support

Hang a picture of a well-established bank, or of your bank, to signify continuous financial support. This is an excellent feng shui tip for those of you who are in business, especially the real-estate or trading businesses, which require good banking support. It is also a good tip for companies that are very highly geared and owe a lot of money to banks. Make certain that the picture of the bank does not have a sharp edge hitting your back, especially if you are the owner, the CEO, or the CFO, since this will constitute a poison arrow hitting you. If you make this kind of mistake, instead of helping you, the picture of the bank building will hurt you.

153 Simulate a mountain behind you

Hang a picture of a high mountain range behind your desk to simulate strong and continuous support from your bosses for your ideas and for your position. If you have a window behind you and you occupy a high-rise building, it can cause you to lose your job or your promotion. Select a picture that does not have water in it. A small waterfall in the middle of huge mountains is acceptable. This tip is particularly suitable for those who are in a career position and whose wellbeing and fortunes depend on their superiors at work. The mountains behind you are a powerful deterrent against office politics.

154 Sloping ceilings are bad news

Avoid sitting in a room with a sloping ceiling. Here the ceiling creates a feeling of imbalance that can cause the energy to become negative. If you cannot do anything about your sloping ceiling, then try to sit under the highest point in the ceiling. If you persist in sitting under a visually low ceiling, it will cause your overall luck to contract. Your position in the office will be undermined and employees who work for you will lose respect for you. This is regarded as a serious affliction for those of you who are in some kind of supervisory or managerial position.

155 Three coins in your purse for luck

Keep three Chinese prosperity coins tied with red cord in your purse or wallet. This is a good way to ensure that you are never short of cash. The coins do not need to be antique coins, but it is a good idea to use Chinese coins, which have a square hole in the center. They invoke the energy of heaven and earth, which then blends with your own human energy to create the unity of tien ti ren. This is one of the fastest ways to create good luck.

156 The double fish symbol

Wear a double fish symbol to protect against financial loss. The double fish is very popular in places like Thailand and Japan, where it is worn as an amulet to protect against being robbed or mugged. Parents believe that children who wear the double fish symbol as a pendant are protected against falling prey to bad people. It is also one of the eight auspicious symbols of Buddhism and is thus very popular among Buddhists.

157 Create a wealth vase

Make your own personal wealth vase and keep it well hidden. First, find a vase that has a fat bottom and a small neck, and then fill it with earth from a rich person's house and cash from a rich man's pocket. This will fill your wealth vase with essential wealth essence. If you wish to stress wealth chi even more, include pictures of the world's richest men and women and images of all the trimmings of wealth, such as mansions, cars, jewelry, and other material goods you would like to possess.

Then fill the vase with nine coins and with cash from nine different countries. You should also fill it with dried foodstuffs tied in tiny plastic bags. Suggested foodstuffs are rice, barley, sorghum, millet, and so forth. Next, you must also include some auspicious symbols of good fortune, such as the god of wealth, ten crystal or lapis globes, three coins tied with red string, and seven types of semi-precious stones.

157

Your wealth vase should be closed with five pieces of square cloth in each of the colors of the five elements (i.e., blue, green, red, yellow, and white). These should be tied tightly with five pieces of string also in the five colors. The vase should then be placed inside a cupboard deep within the household. The vase should never "face" out, so wealth is never given a chance to leave the home. It should never be seen, so your wealth will not invoke jealousy.

158 Sleeping auspiciously

When designing your sleeping feng shui, the most important thing to remember is to try to sleep with your head pointed toward one of your auspicious directions based on your KUA number using the Eight Mansions formula. However, you need to do this while observing the other guidelines on bedroom feng shui, such as having the headboard of your bed placed firmly against a solid wall and making sure there is no toilet on the other side of the wall. You should never sleep with your feet directly pointing to the door, because this is the death position. Nor should there be an exposed overhead beam above you. Bedroom and sleeping feng shui has a very important effect on anyone's luck and well being and it is a good idea to pay extra attention to getting your bedroom feng shui right. You should never place your bed "floating" in the center of the room. Nor should it be placed at an angle to any of the corners. Even when this enables you to sleep in a good direction, the feng shui created is negative. If you are unable to tap even one of your four good directions, it is a good idea to see if you can find another room in the house that allows you to sleep auspiciously.

159 Leafy green plants increase incomes

Display a leafy green plant in the Southeast of your living room or office. The healthier it is, the better. Choose plants that have thick round leaves, such as the jade plant. In fact, the rounder and more water-laden the leaves are, the more auspicious the plants are said to be. Avoid using plants that are spiky or have long, sharp leaves. No matter how pretty they are, anything sharp or knife-like creates poison arrows and you certainly do not want such plants inside the home or in the garden. Make sure you do not place your plant in front of a sharp edge of a column or protruding corner, since it will cause your plant to be hit. When plants placed in the Southeast start to wilt or die, your finances will be adversely affected, and since you are energizing with plants (and not using them as a remedy), it is advisable to use a real rather than a silk plant.

160 Keeping an aquarium

An aquarium of nine goldfish (eight red and one black) in the Southeast is one way to jumpstart your money luck. However, for this water feature to create good feng shui, the aquarium should be kept clean at all times. It is also a very good idea to make sure that the location you have chosen for your aquarium is not afflicted by any of the annual feng shui "afflictions." Make sure the aquarium is not placed on the right-hand side of the main door (from the perspective of inside looking out) because this will cause the man of the house to develop a roving eye. Sometimes this can also cause the man of the house to take a mistress, or worse, a second wife.

161 A toilet on the other side of the wall is bad

If your bed is placed against a wall and there is a toilet on the other side of the wall, it is very bad luck indeed. You should relocate your bed, even if it means tapping a bad luck direction when you sleep.

162 Your prosperity signature

Sign all your important documents using the prosperity signature. This requires you to sign your name with a firm upward stroke when you start and to end with another firm upward stroke. Develop a suitable way of signing and then practice until it becomes perfect. Never sign your name with a final downward stroke. Always end with an optimistic upward stroke—some say the longer, the better. Do not tilt your name to the left, because this suggests falling over backward. Finally, remember that a prosperous signature is always firm and strong and infused with yang chi.

163 Remedy for a missing corner

If any sector of your house is missing, shine a bright light directly on the wall. This has the effect of extending the chi energy beyond, thus correcting the missing corner. A better solution is to install a wall mirror, which has the effect of visually extending the space outward. However, it is important to ensure that the mirror does not reflect anything harmful, such as a toilet, staircase, or long corridor.

164 Cooking with good chi

Ensure that electricity enters your cooking appliances from one of your auspicious directions based on the KUA formula, and especially from your sheng chi direction if you want wealth luck, and from your tien yi direction if you want good health. This was a much easier guideline to follow in the old days when stoves used charcoal and wood for cooking. Then it was easy to determine the "mouth of the stove" and, following that, its facing direction. Today, when gas and electricity are used in ovens, stoves, and other cooking implements, it is harder to determine the "mouth." I have discovered that the correct interpretation is to ensure that the energy being used to cook the food, boil the water, and heat up the foods we eat should come from one of our personal auspicious directions.

165 | # Invite one of the gods of wealth into your home

Display the image of any god of wealth on a table facing the main door. You can select from a pantheon of wealth gods—depending on your own personal preference and on your own cultural heritage and background. The Chinese are fond of several different wealth gods and the most popular is, of course, Tsai Shen Yeh sitting on a tiger and holding an ingot. Other kinds of Choy San include the powerful military wealth gods. Kuan Kung is a firm favorite with many businessmen; he is regarded as a powerful guardian god, and the Nine-Dragon Kuan Kung gives you victory over your competitors.

166 Three-legged toads attract prosperity

Place a three-legged toad under a table or behind a couch in your living room. This little creature is a universal favorite with feng shui enthusiasts around the world mainly because it attracts prosperity vibes into households very efficiently. In recent years, there has been some confusion on where the frog should be facing—in or out of the house. The best place is the corner that is diagonal to the main door, and the frog should be placed looking at the door. If you can, have a few of these auspicious creatures inside your home, hidden under sofas and chairs. It is not necessary to place the three-legged toad high up or on a coffee table. Definitely do not place it on altars on the same level as gods or Buddhas.

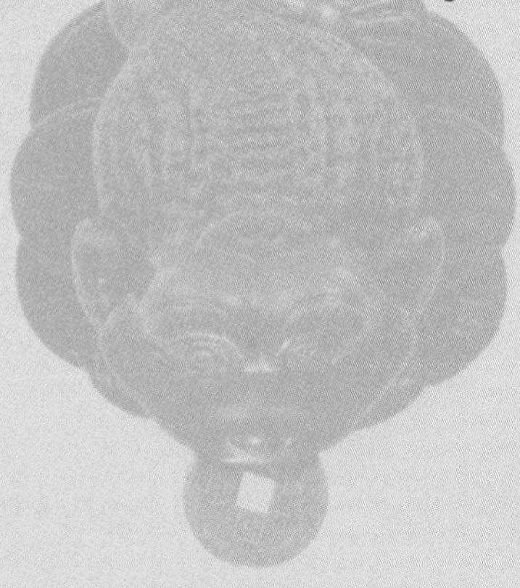

167 "Double" the food in your dining room

Place a wall mirror in the dining room to symbolically double the food served. This is one of the easiest of feng shui enhancers in any household. It is a very effective way of ensuring that the livelihood of the household is adequately protected, enhanced, and improved. When the food served at the dinner table is doubled, it creates the chi of abundance. But do take note that you cannot use this principle of "doubling food" in the kitchen on the assumption that doubling the food being cooked is a good thing. When you place mirrors in the kitchen, it doubles the fire energy, and this can be dangerous. In any case, mirrors in the kitchen have the potential to cause accidents.

168 Have a small-change bank in your West or Northwest corner

Keep small change in a metal container and place this in the West or Northwest. The steady accumulation of coins in these sectors strongly activates the luck signified by these directions. The Northwest is for the luck of helpful people and patronage, while the West brings good descendants and successors. Your piggy bank can also be made of ceramic materials to simulate earth energy, since in the cycle of five elements, earth produces metal.

69 Displaying your rice bowl

Display a golden rice bowl—specially meant for the breadwinner of the family—in the dining room. This tip is especially beneficial for those who love their jobs or professions. When what you do for a living also brings you satisfaction and fulfillment, it is said that you possess the "golden rice bowl," in which case displaying a real golden bowl with golden chopsticks helps to ensure you will never lose your job. Those who dislike their present job should display a golden rice bowl prominently in the dining room to create the vibes for you to land a job you love. Display two sets when there are two breadwinners in the household.

170 Place a money plant on your desk to increase your income

To create the luck of financial success at work, look for a small money or jade plant and place it on the Southeast sector of your desk at work. A real plant will also have the added bonus of creating the growth energy so vital for work success. Make certain the plant stays healthy and sturdy. If it should start to look run down, it is better to change the plant, since weak plants are bad for feng shui.

71 Never store food in garbage containers

It is inauspicious to use plastic "garbage" containers to store your rice, especially when rice is the staple food of your household. This applies also to your other foods, such as bread or dried noodles. When you want good fortune, it is most important to safeguard the staple food that sustains you. The symbolic meaning transcends spatial chi, so your feng shui and well being will be affected. Even when your daily intake of rice is very small, invest in an auspicious rice container.

172 Select an auspicious container for your staple food

Always store your rice or bread inside an auspicious container with lucky symbols. Some of the auspicious emblems to look for are longevity and double happiness symbols. Containers do not need to be too big, but they should also not be excessively small. Most important is that they should appear solid and precious-looking.

73 Place a red packet inside your rice urn

Place a red packet filled with real money deep inside your rice urn; at the bottom is best. This simulates the accumulation of wealth for the household. This tip works best when you faithfully "add" to your wealth by adding an extra and new red packet each year. Let the amount that you place inside the red packet grow from one year to the next, because this will ensure that family assets appreciate in value from year to year.

174 Good feng shui for your rice urn

Keep your rice urn covered and never allow it to get more than half empty. But first, do ensure that you select your family rice urn with care. For good luck, the family rice urn should be made of either ceramic or another earth-related material. Any other element is usually not as auspicious. So avoid metal, wood, or plastic containers. Look for containers with auspicious or longevity symbols or other decorative images that have good feng shui meaning.

175 Electronics are best placed in the West or Northwest

Electronic equipment such as television sets and computers is beneficial when placed in the West or Northwest of your living or sitting room in the home or along the Northwest wall of the office. This has the effect of energizing the metal element chi of these sectors, which benefits the father of the family as well as the children. Photocopy and fax machines have the effect of activating chi energy wherever they are placed, so the general rule is that they should be placed in sectors of the office with favorable Flying Stars and should never be placed in sectors with the quarrelsome number 3 star. In this connection, it is useful to familiarize yourself with the annual Flying Star charts in order to avoid such things as high turnover of staff, quarrels in the office, and obstacles caused by unfriendly authorities who give you a hard time.

176 Create "happy water"

When you build or introduce water features around the home to activate happiness and prosperity luck, make sure the water is kept "happy." Do refrain from shouting, fighting, and quarreling in the vicinity of your water features. One of the highest selling books in Japan, written by a Japanese professor, describes how water can reveal whether or not it is balanced and happy. When "good" water is frozen into ice, and then photographed, it shows beautifully balanced crystal formations. Sad and disturbed water, on the other hand, displays unbalanced and hazy crystal formations. So when you keep fish in your water, make certain the water is kept clean and that your fish are happy. This ensures they emit happy energy into the water, which in turn attracts good fortune.

177 Make your dining table auspicious

A well-enhanced dining table brings good eating luck, which always spells prosperity. This is why you will find that the wealthy Chinese always invest in well-made and well-decorated circular or rectangular dining tables. Round tables bring heaven luck, while rectangular tables bring growth luck. In addition, dining tables are almost always made of very hard wood such as blackwood or rosewood, and they are almost always decorated with auspicious images (fish, bats, longevity signs, and so forth) engraved in beautiful rainbow-colored mother of pearl. All these make for auspicious dining, which plays a large part in gaining good feng shui.

178 Watch how you sit when you eat

Never sit directly facing a door when you eat. Nor should you sit directly facing a staircase or a long corridor. The ideal situation would be for you to sit facing one of your personal good directions while at the same time observing the basic tenets of feng shui. So do not directly face anything sharp or protruding, or position yourself directly under an exposed overhead structural beam.

179 Avoid water features in the bedroom

Water features in your bedroom will cause loss of wealth and also create marriage problems that could cause a permanent rift between the couple. Here, the reference to water refers to aquariums and small decorative water features such as rolling crystal balls and other crystal with water formations. It does not refer to drinking water. Paintings that depict small brooks and streams are harmless, but a picture of a large waterfall such as Niagara Falls can be dangerous. It will cause sleepless nights and introduce discord between an otherwise loving couple.

180 Reflect good views into your home

To capture wealth luck, install a mirror to reflect a good view of water into your home. This has the effect of "capturing" wealth into the home. In fact, if you can literally extend and expand your home to encircle a water pond that was outside the house and now bring it into the house this brings new wealth to the family. It is a rule that once a house has been built you should never dig a pond inside the house, but if you "embrace" an external pond and bring it in, then you have effectively captured new-found wealth.

181 Flow of water past the house

For houses facing secondary directions, water should flow from right to left from your viewpoint of inside looking out. For houses facing primary directions, water should flow from left to right. If there is a large drain outside the house that has the water flowing in the wrong direction past the house, you should block the view of water from your main door.

182 Never let anyone step on your company name

Do not place your company name on a floor mat, thereby causing people to step on your name. This brings bad luck to the company and, over time, causes loss and a dwindling of profits.

183 Enhancing your floor mat

Tape three Chinese prosperity coins energized with red cord under your floor mat. This suggests that you are stepping on "gold" each time you enter or leave the house or office. But never, ever place your name or your company name or logo on the floor mat, because this means that you and others will be stepping on them. I am often appalled when I enter some big-name brand shops and find I am stepping on their name as I enter. I am thus seldom surprised when I read eventually of the demise of the brand. So, enhance your floor mat, but never label it with your name.

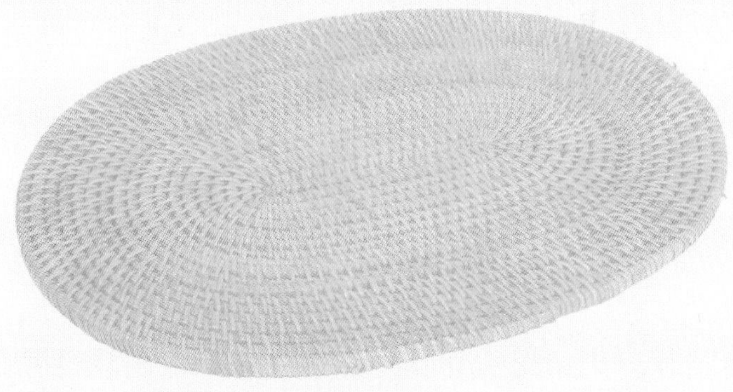

184 No mirrors in kitchens

Mirrors reflecting the cooking fire cause accidents and problems for young children. It is simply just such bad luck to have mirrors in the kitchen, especially if the mirror reflects the stove. This can sometimes cause the breadwinner to have a very bad accident.

185 Keep creeping plants under control

A front door or gate engulfed by a creeping plant indicates that you will lose your home. Even worse, if the front wall of your house is completely taken over by an aggressively creeping parasitic plant, you will find that residents within the home will feel perpetually tired and lacking in energy. If you really must have a creeper, do keep it under control. In this connection, I want to warn you against the banyan tree, which grows so fast that before you know, it its very strong roots have taken hold of your home if you allow them too near. If you see a banyan tree growing on your wall, it is best to remove it or to pot it.

186 Potpourris are not good feng shui

It is because feng shui does not encourage the use of dried plants that the attitude toward so-called fragrant potpourri is also negative. Having pots of scented dried herbs or leaves is like having a bowl of dirt on the table and is thus not auspicious. They are, however, quite acceptable when placed inside bathrooms.

87 Dried flowers create bad chi

Never use dried flowers because they signify death as well as excessive yin energy. Dried plants are in reality dead and they are ready to turn into dust. Displaying them on table tops or mixed with fresh flowers brings bad luck to the whole room. Better to use fake plants than dried plants.

188 Artificial plants are OK

Artificial silk plants work as well as real ones, if the purpose is to deflect the sharp edge of walls and corners or to block adverse views from sight. They are less effective when you need plants to enhance wood corners. Then real plants are needed to generate the growth chi required. Whether you use real or silk plants, always make sure they are kept clean at all times.

189 A jade plant brings abundance

A flowering jade plant near your front door attracts prosperity and abundance, although these plants do not flower frequently. Many believe the plant itself is already so auspicious that when it blooms it is a bonus. Jade plants have thick succulent leaves that resemble small pieces of imperial jade.

190 Water and trees on rooftop gardens

Rooftop gardens must not have any water features or large trees. Those of you living in penthouses should take special note of this warning on water. In feng shui, the element of water flows downward and water at the top of a hill is considered dangerous—in situations where it overflows, the water will bring terrible disaster. In fact, according to the I Ching, water on top of mountain is one of the four danger signs. As for trees, when they grow too big, their roots are said to symbolically stifle you.

191 A meandering path to your front door

Place nine round stepping-stones along a meandering path leading toward your front door. This is a favorite Taoist feng shui recommendation, because it is believed that the nine-coin image is a powerful sign of wealth. This tip is closely allied to having nine emperor coins tied with red thread inside your wallet to ensure continuous availability of money.

192 The purifying energy of salt

One way of cleaning house energy is to mop the entire house with salt water. What you need is rock salt or sea salt—these are natural salts and they have tremendous cleansing power. Get a pound of salt, melt it in hot water, then use the salt water to clean all the surfaces inside the home. This kind of salt water is especially good at getting rid of negative energy. It is also a good way of spiritually cleansing any antique items such as furniture, cabinets, or decorative images that you may have recently purchased for the house.

193 Fruiting lime trees bring "gold"

A pair of lime trees flanking your main door invites good luck into your home. This is because the fruit of the lime tree not only signifies abundance and prosperity, but its sour taste is also able to absorb and kill any bad luck or evil influence that may have been disturbing your home without your knowledge. Lime fruits work a little like salt—they soak up bad energy, hence cleansing your home while attracting abundance.

194 A lime-fruit cleansing ritual

It is believed that when you feel down and depressed, or suspect that someone is sending bad vibes toward you, one sure way of getting rid of invisible but harmful energy is to get two lime fruits and clutch one in each of your hands. Then close your fingers over the fruit and press and rotate the fruit inside your clenched fingers. Imagine that whatever bad energy is afflicting you is being sucked into the lime fruits in your hands. All bad energy is flowing into the fruits. After about five minutes, find a flow of water (a drain or a river) and throw the limes behind your shoulder into the water flow and, without looking back, walk away. This will rid you of all bad luck.

195 | Take a salt bath

If you have recently visited someone in the hospital, attended a funeral, or been involved in any situation that required you to enter into a building where yin energy prevails—such as a prison, police station, or courtroom—it is advisable to give yourself a salt bath when you return. Use rock salt or sea salt and wash your hair with lime water. These rituals are believed to ensure that any lingering negative energy is washed away before it has a chance to stick to your home. This is one of the most basic ways of safeguarding the chi energy of your home.

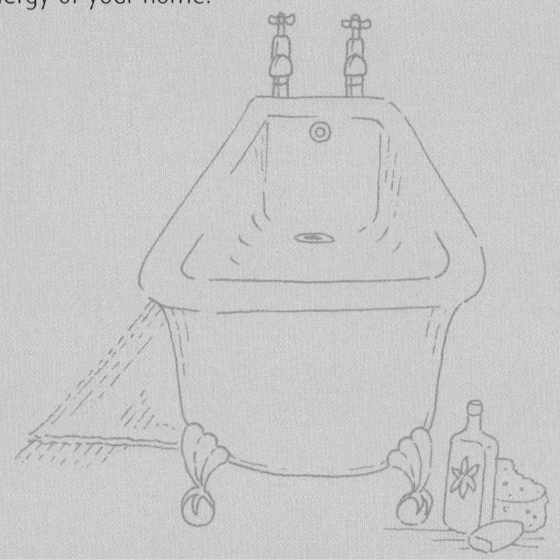

196 | Space can be stylish

Just because you incorporate feng shui into your home design does not mean you cannot have a stylish space. You can, if you practice feng shui with a practical attitude, allowing your own common sense, style, and preferences to dictate the enhancers and remedies you use and how you use them. It is not necessary to use Chinese images if these do nothing for you. The important thing is to understand the essence of feng shui and the symbolic meanings of objects, colors, and elements.

197 Placement of garages

A garage in front of your main door is not a good thing because this obstructs inward-flowing chi. If you have a special covered roof area in front of the main door, where cars can drive in to drop you off, make sure you do not keep your car in that space. If you do, your car will be blocking your luck, and since cars are made of metal, the energy is unyielding. Not a good situation.

198 Round pond in North sector for career luck

A round pond in the North sector of your garden will bring excellent career luck. This is because the circular shape indicates metal energy and metal produces water. Since water is the element of the North, and since the North sector signifies career luck, a round pond here enhances career aspirations. Just make certain that the water stays clean at all times.

199 Fresh flowers bring good feng shui

Fresh flowers in the South, Southeast, or East sectors of your desk or room signify strong growth energy. Fresh flowers are always good feng shui because they emit precious yang energy into your space. But always throw them out at the first sign of fading. The worst thing you can do is to have flowers that are rotting in a vase filled with smelly, dirty water. In fact, you should really change the water every day to keep it fresh and clean.

200 Carp with a single red dot

If you have children of school or college age you should not keep any koi fish with a single red dot on its forehead in your pond. This is widely regarded to be the mark of failure. According to legend, all carp that successfully jump over the Dragon gate become Dragons, while those that fail have a red dot stamped on their forehead. The Dragon gate signifies the imperial examinations and the Dragons signify those who successfully pass the exams and go on to become important officials in the emperor's court.

201 Making your cash register lucky

To increase business turnover, position a large mirror to reflect the cash register. This has the effect of symbolically "doubling" the money you collect each day. If you place auspicious wealth symbols such as coins and ingots near your cash register, it encourages money to flow toward it.

202 Unify your feng shui

Many people find the different feng shui formulas to be confusing—and indeed, they are so, especially when there seem to be apparent contradictions in their respective methods. The key is to unify the look of your home so that it seamlessly incorporates all the basic fundamentals of feng shui. This means identifying all the auspicious corners of the home based on the different methods and then choosing the corners that also correspond to your personalized good luck directions, based on the Eight Mansions KUA formula method. This way, you unify what is good for you with what is also good for the house and for everyone else.

203 Keep the five elements in mind

It is really important to keep the five elements and their three cycles of interaction in mind when doing any kind of feng shui—this is because ultimately it is the five elements that will help you determine the compatibility of the way you have designed your space. When you bring the elements together, you will be able to achieve a harmonizing of shapes, lights, colors, and materials that will create the ambience of good feng shui.

204 Use the productive cycle to harmonize

Use the productive cycle of element relationships when designing the feng shui of rooms. For instance, a room in the North corner of your home belongs to the element of water and if you want to enhance this corner, then choosing a predominantly blue color scheme is helpful. White is even better, because white is metal, which produces water. The shape of metal is round; hence circular objects in this room would be good feng shui. Another example: if the room is located in the Southeast of the house, this means the element of its chi is wood. Here, a predominantly green color would work, but blue, which is of the water element, is even better, because water produces wood.

205 ## Maintain good balance of yin and yang

While there are all sorts of guidelines to follow in feng shui, it is always a good idea to ensure that a good balance of yin and yang energy is maintained at all times. This means that rooms should not be allowed to get too noisy or be too silent. There should be no areas in the home that get too dark during the day, nor should there be parts of the home that are not occupied at all. This will create an imbalance of energy, which makes it difficult for a good flow of chi. And then the chi simply stagnates and gets stale.

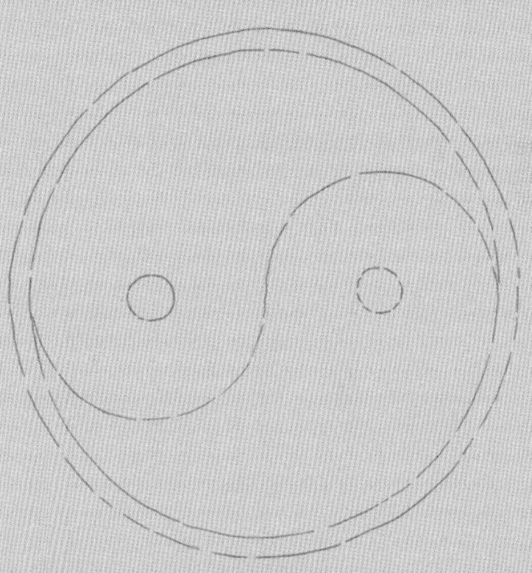

206 Throw out chipped glasses and cups

There is nothing worse than drinking coffee from a chipped cup or eating dinner from a nearly broken plate. Chinese matriarchs are strict about this. So never allow chipped tableware to be used. Throw it away as soon as there's a crack, even if it's just a hairline one. When visiting someone and you are served from a chipped cup, my advice is to politely decline to drink from it, because it will cause bad luck to befall you.

207 Bad vibes from antique furniture

Be very careful about installing antique furniture in your home, and especially your bedroom. If you sleep on an old antique bed or live with an antique cabinet, you should always wipe the furniture thoroughly with rock or sea salt first. This will help you get rid of any bad vibrations that may be stuck to the furniture. Usually, the harder the wood, the denser it is, and here is where hundreds of years of old energy will be stuck to it. If the energy is good energy, things are fine, but if it is bad, then you are sure to be affected. So do cleanse all your antique furniture. If you haven't yet, it is never too late to do so. Make sure you clean the inside as well. Placing a sachet of salt inside an old cabinet is also a good idea.

208 Be extra careful with tight corners

Negative energy tends to build up in the tight corners of your space, so do pay some attention to these corners in your home. Be particularly mindful of the corner that is diagonally opposite your front door—this is one of the most important corners of the home, for it is here that good luck chi tends to settle and accumulate. In other words, use that corner and benefit from its auspicious chi energy—don't imprison that corner with a big piece of furniture. In fact, at least once a month or as regularly as you can, let energy flow through cramped spaces such as narrow hallways and little store areas by opening all doors and windows.

209 Do not overdo your decorating

There is no need to overdo the decorating of corners, either. When you read about so many things being good for this corner or that corner and they all look so tempting that you really cannot resist, you should. It is always better to keep a firm rule of not more than three energizers in any single corner. If in the course of the year you get tired of any of your decorative objects, you can change them for some other energizer. There is no need to go over the top, although having said that, I am one of those who has a tendency always to go over the top. I have to confess it has not harmed me so far, but the space I have to work with is rather large, so I guess I can get away with it. Balance is the key, really.

210 Clearing clutter beats the blues

One of the easiest ways to practice instant feng shui is by clearing clutter in the home. Over time, the stuff in any home will have become thick with stale and stagnant chi that sticks to unmoved and unused furniture, closets, and cabinets. This causes residents to get trapped in a downward spiral of depression. Part of the reason is that the energy around them gets too heavy and weighs them down. To beat the blues, all you need to do is to start moving stuff around. Awaken the chi by moving and rearranging the furniture, in the process clearing out junk that you had long forgotten. As you work, the energy lightens and chi gets freer. This is a great way to beat the blues.

211 | Staircase feng shui is important

It is common to ignore the staircases of homes and yet these are conduits of chi energy. The staircase is where energy flows from the ground to the first level, so make sure your staircases are never blocked with books, boxes, newspapers, and so forth. Make sure the chi is able to flow freely up and down. If you like, you can hang pictures on the walls of the staircase to slow down the flow of chi—this is always a good thing to do.

212 What do you have under the staircase?

It is incredibly important that you do not place anything that means a lot to you under the staircase for everyone to step on several times daily. For instance, never place your important files and documents under the stairs, and refrain from placing your children's school books, school bag, or even worse, the study table under a staircase. This is such bad feng shui! If you have the Fuk Luk Sau or Kuan Kung image under the staircase, then instead of bringing good luck, the disrespect implied could well boomerang against you. So my advice is to keep the area under the stairs free of anything.

213 Water under the stairs hurts the children

It may indeed be very beautiful to create a landscaped pond under your staircase, but if you do this, you will be creating extreme misfortune luck for the children of the house. The deeper the water, the more severe the misfortune, so do refrain from doing this. Instead of water, it is a good idea to keep the bottom of staircases well lit. You can, if you wish, have a store room here, but do not keep important and memorable things here, such as treasured photographs or your safe. Instead, use it to keep mops, brooms, and other unimportant items.

214 Eight steps to revitalize your home

Your home needs a shot of fresh new energy and this can be done through a massive decluttering exercise. Doing so allows you to synchronize with the new period 8. Here is an eight-step plan to revitalize your home:

1. Make a list of things that need to be done within a specified time frame.

2. Get organized by identifying what you want to do with each room.

3. Get started—begin with the easiest room to declutter and revitalize.

4. Select a room to be a "halfway room" to place unwanted stuff in while deciding what you wish to throw away, what you need to repair, and what you decide to sell.

5. Buy trash bags to contain all your new-found "rubbish."

6. Revitalize with a fresh coat of paint.

7. Invest in some new lights and maybe one new door or new windows.

8. Finally, let new wind (a gentle breeze) flow right through the house by opening several doors or windows.

215 Unblock pathways to your main door

If you want good feng shui and want your life to move along smoothly, you should make a real effort to keep your main door free of physical obstacles—closets, boxes, and so forth. Only then can good positive chi enter and flow unimpeded through your home. The door is where you, your spirit, and the spirit of your home move in and out. This flow of chi should never be blocked. If it is, your life also gets blocked and projects that you're working on could get stymied and delayed, with all kinds of obstacles standing in the way. Relationships could start to flounder and upward mobility at your job could come to a grinding halt. So do unblock pathways that lead to the door. This applies both inside and outside the house.

216 Treat bedrooms as sacred space

Your bedroom will bring you good health and good feng shui if you treat it as a place of rest. It should be free of clutter, so make it a point to dispose of old newspapers, magazines, old cans, and so forth. At your dressing table, clear out old makeup and creams. The bedroom is where you are the most vulnerable. When you sleep, you are in another realm of existence, so keep this space sacred and special. At all costs, keep out negative energies from the bedroom.

217 Clean up your closet

Your closets should be kept clean and up to date, so that when you visit it each morning, it becomes a source of happiness chi. Practice the 80/20 rule by throwing out twenty percent of your wardrobe each year—give old clothes to charity and make way for new clothes to come into your life. This is the secret of moving on to fresh new beginnings each year. Unless you make room by clearing out some old stuff, new clothes—and by extension new experiences—will never come into your life. Besides, it is a very good practice to share some of your possessions with those who are less fortunate than you.

218 Always fall asleep with a smile on your face

Never go to bed feeling unhappy or depressed. Make an effort to bring a smile to your face just before you sleep. This is a powerful secret, which a holy yogic once passed to me. He told me that when we go to sleep happy, it brings happy dreams and enhances the quality of our sleep. I have followed this small tip for several years now with amazing success—so remember, the best thing you can do for a loved one is to ensure they do not go to sleep feeling depressed, or unhappy, or angry. Whatever is troubling or bothering them should be resolved before they sleep. And if you are nursing someone who is about to pass away, make a real effort to make him or her feel happy. Buddhists believe that when someone dies angry, the propelling karma will cause them to have a difficult rebirth.

219 Bedroom taboos

Here is a checklist of things not to do or have in the bedroom:

• Do not have your exercise equipment in the bedroom. Your place of rest is not your gym. Worse yet if you have a wall mirror.

• Do not store anything on elevated shelves directly above the bed. These create weight above the sleeping body, which signifies some burden.

• Keep all work-related junk, computers, and files out of the bedroom—these will only transfer stress into your psyche.

• Do not place junk under or over your bed.

• Keep the space in front of the door clear of obstacles.

• Keep questionable art out of the bedroom. Avoid water scenes, wild animal prints, or paintings of anything that looks even remotely hostile.

220 Removing negative chi from neighbors

Hostile chi from neighbors may be relatively harmless caused by frivolous gossip and some small-minded envy. This can be ignored. At other times the energy from next door can be merely annoying, such as when there are kids whose screaming and fighting drives you up the wall. Their childish antics may disturb and aggravate you. Overcoming this kind of energy is easy. Just place a large urn of water with a wide mouth and narrow base between your home and the neighbor's house.

When the energy being sent your way is bitter or hateful, you may want to counter it with stronger measures. There are many ways to protect yourself, and the Chinese believe the best way is to use a round mirror circled by trigrams arranged like a yin pa kua symbol. This powerful tool bounces back a thousand-fold whatever energy is being sent your way. But unless the aggravation is really severe do not use this drastic cure. Instead, use a small brass mirror directly reflecting your neighbor's house. Hanging some happy bells between the two homes will energize friendship chi.

221 Minimalist chic or not—its your call

Feng shui rooms can be very minimalist or they can look very "loud and decorated." Young people of today do not like their homes to be crowded with too many decorative objects. There are no prescribed rules in feng shui interior decoration. You can be as creative as you wish, but no matter how minimal or how loud you are, always take note of the orientations of rooms, so you will instantly know when the elements are in harmony and when they conflict.

Never allow the elements of each corner to get "killed or destroyed" by the placement of something belonging to a destructive element. Do not place plants in the Northeast and Southwest—let earth energy dominate here. Do not place water in the South—fire energy must dominate here. And in the West and Northwest, which are metal corners, too many lights could be harmful. In the Southeast and East, where wood is the ruling element, go easy on the metal. Finally, in the North, which is the place of water energy, be careful about placing excessive rocks and boulders, because earth destroys water. So let your style of décor dominate, but let feng shui be your guide.

222 Keep purses free of clutter

A woman's purse is the ultimate store of junk—receipts, credit card slips, odd pieces of note paper, business cards, old lipsticks, reminder pads, keys, pens, pencils, and all sorts of memorabilia such as letters, photographs, etc... truly an amazing collection of clutter. It is a good idea to undertake a spring clean of your purse at least once a month. This way, the chi energy associated with your finances and well being never has a chance to become stagnant.

223 Red wallet brings good cash flow

To create the luck of constantly flowing money so you never run out of cash, use a bright red wallet. Laminated or patent red leather that has a shiny surface is the best. And then inside the wallet keep three coins tied with red string to accumulate yang energy. If you can keep some change from a rich man or woman's pocket to "borrow" some of his or her wealth chi, it will be even better. However, do make certain that your wallet never gets tainted with "bad money," i.e., money that is stolen or obtained through foul means.

224 Make your space sparkle

When your spaces are dirt-free and fresh-smelling, and tabletops and floors sparkling with cleanliness, the energy of the house is likewise pure and uplifting. When you read about how space clearing improves the feng shui of any house, it applies as much to physical dirt as it does to intangible dirt. Clean homes are happy homes. This may sound obvious, but unless a conscious effort is made to ensure this, you will be surprised at how fast the dirt piles up. Bathrooms and toilets are the most obvious places for energy to get polluted, so do make a special effort here to make sure the rest of the house does not absorb the negative vibes.

225 Think visually

It is useful to plan your feng shui—placement of doors, arrangement of furniture, the flow of human traffic through the spaces of your home—on paper. Working from a floor layout plan is one of the most efficient ways of planning how you wish to implement your own feng shui measures, but you must also think visually. For example, a wall mirror is only a line but in reality you should always ask yourself what a mirror reflects; the same with steps and multilevel floors—these are three-dimensional features that require you to think visually. If you can develop this ability to think visually, you will find that your practice of feng shui improves significantly.

226 Throw out the clichés

There are a number of decorative clichés and color schemes that simply do not work from a feng shui perspective, so anything that runs counter to feng shui principles should be axed. Examples are long corridors, doors directly facing each door, three doors in a straight line, facing a three-way intersection, and also things that are asymmetrical—in feng shui terms these are deemed to be unbalanced. Feng shui does seem to favor structures, furniture placements, lines, and angles that are balanced. In this context, "modern abstract art" should be viewed with some wariness.

227 Make your home feng shui unique

The way to create good feng shui in any home is to systematically get rid of sharp objects and disarm poison arrows, keep the space clean and free of clutter, and ensure a continuous and smooth flow of chi at all times. When every corner of every room of your home appears well-used and properly lit, with no dark, sad corners, your home becomes unique in the energy that it radiates. Usually, the sound of running water turned on for 24 hours a day adds amazing chi energy.

228 Select only auspicious paintings

If you like displaying paintings inside your home, choose them with some thought and care. Avoid abstract paintings that suggest hostility, or those that display angular and sharp lines. Most definitely, avoid paintings of fierce animals and birds, especially if they are predatory. It is also a good idea not to hang sad paintings that depict the ravages of war or hunger, in the mistaken belief that these make you more socially conscious. There is nothing more harmful to the energy of the home than to have sad, frightened faces hanging on the walls. Instead, hang happy paintings of auspicious animals such as horses, elephants, fish, and tortoises. It is also a good idea to hang paintings of birds—but keep them friendly and reject those that look fearsome or hostile.

229 Create a stunning centerpiece

It is good feng shui when you have an auspicious centerpiece in your living room that seems to emanate good energy. This can be a brightly lit sculpture, or, as in my case, a huge crystal ball. I have had it on my coffee table for twenty years now and with a light shining on it, this crystal is like a source of energy radiating outward. It creates good feng shui when the crystal is pure and imbued with positive energy. Other suitable centerpieces can be symbols that mean something special to you. In recent months, I have placed a pair of ammonite shell fossils on the coffee table of my other living room. These too are objects that radiate energy outward into the room. Once again, to emphasize its positive energy, I shine a bright light on it for at least three hours each day.

230 Don't sit under a ceiling fan

Never sit directly below a ceiling fan, because the chi of fast-moving air can be negative. This also represents hostile blades threatening you from above. If you want to have a breeze in your room, it is better to use wall or floor fans. Air conditioners directly above you or your bed are also not a good idea, because this signifies something hostile over you as you sleep.

231 Doors should open inward

Doors and gates should open inward to welcome good fortune into the home. This is a great deal more auspicious than doors opening outward. At the same time, there should never be anything that blocks your door as it opens. When doors are blocked, this signifies obstacles to all your projects. Doors should also not be placed in an awkward manner—this causes the flow of chi to move in an awkward fashion. Pay particular attention to the main door into your home.

232 Activate good feng shui for your telephone

Attach three coins energized with red thread to your telephone to increase sales. If you are a frequent user of cell phones (who isn't these days?), then look for auspicious phone holders to ensure that all your calls bring opportunities and good news. Activating your telephone is a modern interpretation of feng shui.

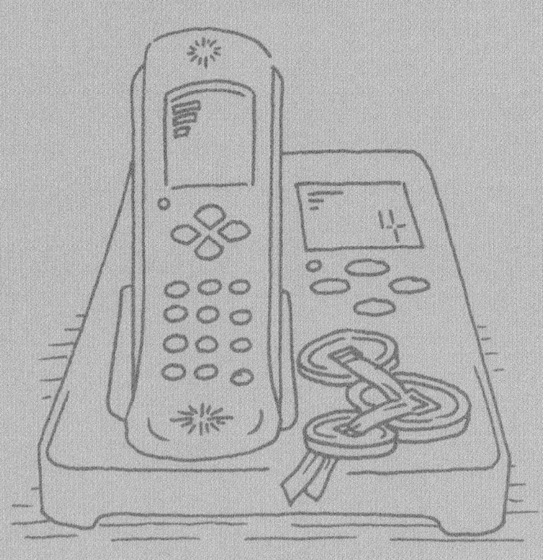

233 Develop your own space magic

Spatial feng shui is really akin to creating magic with your space—it has to do with happiness vibrations. If each morning before you go to work, your space is filled with happy music that also puts you into a good mood, this will ensure the energy created at sunrise is positive. Remember that the time between 7:am and 9:am is the time of the Dragon, so if you personally create happy chi, it will set the tone for the rest of the day. Remember that when we deal with energy, we humans are the greatest and most potent of power sources.

234 Water should flow inward... never out

Water features should always flow toward the house and should never appear to be flowing outward. This denotes the flow of family wealth outward. Sometimes you might even lose your home. It is the same in corporate buildings. When you have a water feature near the main entrance, such as a single-tier waterfall, it should not appear to be flowing outward. When water flows outward, the owner of the building is almost certain to lose it eventually. Residents within also suffer a lessening of their incomes and wealth.

235 Beware of toilets in the Southeast

Toilets located in the Southeast of your home will flush away your money luck. This is because the Southeast is the sector of the house that represents wealth luck, and you could find your business suffering and your profits affected. If you have a toilet in the Southeast, hang a wind chime inside the bathroom, or place something metallic. The wind chime is good, because in creating the sound of metal, it is releasing yang metal energy.

236 A lamp in the Southwest brings love

Place a round, yellow, or red lamp in the Southwest and turn it on every night for forty-nine nights to activate your love luck. This is one of the best ways of energizing to attract love into your life. You can augment it by placing a pair of mandarin ducks carved out of rose quartz in the love corner. This can be the Southwest or it can be the corner that corresponds to your nien yen direction.

237 Crystal to enhance the Southwest

To energize universal love energy, place a raw crystal in the Southwest. A rose quartz crystal is particularly energizing for romantic happiness. To attract wealth and prosperity in a relationship, you might consider placing a citrine crystal in the Southeast and for love that is romantic and loving place an amethyst crystal. These are only some ideas. In truth, all crystals have some auspicious meanings and attract some positive attributes. You can also use your own instincts to select the kind of crystals that you feel an affinity for.

238 Thorny red roses can ruin relationships

Never give your date or someone you care for a dozen thorny, deep red roses or it will mean a quick end to your love relationship. According to feng shui experts, red flowers often signify the death of a relationship and in some cases, they can also signify the death of a loved one. Red flowers with thorns are doubly unlucky. Stick to "safe" colors like yellow, peach, or pink blooms. If you send roses, do make sure you remove the thorns.

239 Best flowers for a date

On a date, bring your sweetheart fresh violet-colored orchids, thorn-free yellow roses, or creamy magnolias. There are so many auspicious flowers such as peonies and chrysanthemums that one is simply spoiled for choice. Select colors that blend well with the KUA element of the recipient. So if his or her KUA number is 1, 3, or 4 for instance, send blue or lavender flowers. If 9, send pink or peach blooms. If 6, 7, 2, or 8, send yellow flowers.

240 Tap your nien yen direction for love luck

On a romantic date, try to sit facing your nien yen direction, which is your personal love and marriage direction under the Eight Mansions KUA formula on personalized directions. Sit facing your nien yen direction at all times to enhance chances of romance coming into your life. For good measure, also sleep with your head pointed to the nien yen direction.

241 Unsuitable gifts for a love relationship

You should never give anyone a gift of something sharp or pointed, because it causes very bad energy between the two of you. Examples of unsuitable gifts are scissors, knives, letter openers, and even nail manicure sets. If your loved one or a good friend gives you something unsuitable like this, you should immediately give him or her a bank note to "buy" the gift symbolically. Do the same for a gift of a watch or a clock, since according to the Chinese, these gifts are said to be inauspicious.

242 Wear the double happiness symbol

Wear the double happiness symbol in the form of jewelry or motifs on your clothes to bring you great marriage luck! This is probably the most powerful of the love symbols. But do note, however, that it does denote marriage, so those who are not ready for commitment should not use the symbol. In feng shui, there is no room for frivolous one-night stands—love and romance is always equated with marriage and family. This is the wholesomeness of feng shui, which is so assuring.

243 Double happiness inside the bedroom

The double happiness symbol is a very potent symbol of marital bliss, so displaying it inside your bedroom has the power to re-energize a marriage that has gone stale or where boredom seems to have set in. The double happiness sign is best carved onto beds or hung up as a picture—it is like hanging a strong affirmation in the bedroom to create happiness energy. When the sign is also lit up, it becomes a lot stronger.

244 Yang chi reignites passion

Brighten up the bedroom you share with your lover with cheerful splashes of yang color (red or yellow) to re-light the passion! When boredom sets in, it usually reflects the creeping dominance of yin chi and this is easily countered with lights, sounds, or activity. Sometimes, just bringing the radio into the bedroom can make a real difference if there has been too much stillness and non-activity inside the bedroom. If this does not work, look for a young boy under the age of nine and get him to roll over the marital bed. If he is a Dragon child, it is even better—the idea is to create a massive quantity of pure yang energy inside the bedroom, and there is nothing purer than a young child.

245 Avoid a ceiling fan above the bed

Do not place your bed directly below a whirling ceiling fan. The fan churns up energy when you are sleeping and it disturbs both of you. When you sleep under a fan, the chi cuts into the sleeping couple, causing them to grow apart. Better to install a silent air conditioner somewhere away from the marital bed and remove the fan altogether. This is a serious affliction and you should try to have the fan removed.

246 Keep wood chi out of the bedroom

Keep fresh flowers and green plants out of the bedroom because they can cause problems between the couple. The growth chi of fresh plants is unsuitable and incompatible with the bedroom. It is even worse if these plants are cacti or have thorns and spikes in them. If you do not throw them out they could cause you to lose each other, and also cause you to be depleted of your yang essence.

247 Banish TV sets from the bedroom

Avoid having television sets and computers in the bedroom because their screens have reflective surfaces that act like mirrors when turned off. If you have them, at least make sure that they do not directly face the bed. If they do, make sure that you cover the screen when you fall asleep. The excessive yang energy produced by televisions and computers in the bedroom can cause strain and tension in your relationship with your partner.

248 Pictures of women in bedrooms cause problems

Remove all pictures of females from the bedroom. This includes glamorous women, paintings of nudes, and so forth. Their presence makes a marriage crowded. It is a strong affliction, which hurts the marriage. Pictures of naked women inside bedrooms hurt both the husband and the wife.

249 **Never point a finger directly at someone**

Never point a knife, a fork, or your index finger at your loved one, and for that matter at anyone, because it is rude as well as being very negative and will create friction and bad feng shui between you almost immediately! It is like sending a poison arrow outward. When someone does it to you, it is important to immediately turn away so that you are no longer in the "line of fire." Or better yet, use your hand to push the energy away from you symbolically. With palm facing outward, push the air outward three times.

250 Water in the bedroom causes all kinds of misfortune

Never, ever place any water features in the bedroom because this will cause a loss of something or someone you love. This means you could lose some money, get burgled or robbed, or worse, lose someone dear to you. Water inside the bedroom means a water feature—it does not mean a glass of water or a flask of water. This taboo is especially important to note if your bedroom is located in the South sector of your house.

251 Lady with the flute

Hang a painting of a young woman wearing traditional silks and playing a flute or any other kind of romantic instrument in your living room. This is believed to symbolically send out the enticing notes that attract harmony chi into any home. A lady playing the flute is also believed to be an excellent symbol for the marriage of residents to be happy and fulfilled. The Chinese believe that the sound of the flute is very soothing and is enticing for the good sheng chi. In the old days, beautiful maidens were taught to play the flute at the court of the emperor.

252 Rose quartz crystals for love luck

Get a pink rose quartz crystal heart and display it in the Southwest corner of your home to activate your love luck. Like the boulders placed outside the home in the garden, pink rose quartz crystals activate the romantic chi of the space. Pink rose quartz are the gemstones associated with love and romance, so using anything made with this gemstone—gem trees, mandarin ducks, carvings, pebbles—and placing them in the Southwest brings love luck.

253 Love affirmations and photographs

Stick red love or mystic knots on pictures of you and your partner to create smooth love chi between you. This is like sticking positive affirmations about your love for each other. Look for picture frames that suggest love and togetherness with which to frame your pictures and then have them around your home. This will symbolically strengthen both of you as a couple. There is nothing like love affirmations to keep the relationship strong. Wedding pictures should also be hung up in the house and these should ideally face the good directions of the husband.

254 Enhancing love and marriage chi

Display a pair of mandarin ducks or flying geese in your nien yen corner to enhance love and marriage luck. Paired love birds are very powerful love symbols because birds are not only considered to be symbols of loving togetherness, they are also known as messengers of the gods. When you display bird images in the home, they always bring good fortune and as a pair, they are good for the marriage and the family.

255 Sending a wish to the Sky Dragon

Write a wish on a red or yellow helium balloon and release it in the wind to find the mate of your dreams! This has always been a very popular Taoist ritual, which is effective for realizing your deepest aspirations. So if a mate is what you want, writing the wish on the balloon and sending it skyward is an effective way of having it manifest itself in your life soon. The balloon wish ritual can be applied to any aspiration—but remember to write your name and address on the balloon and stick to one wish per balloon.

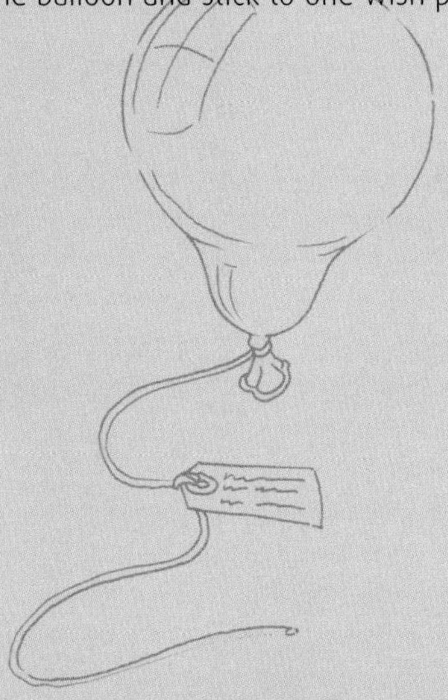

256 Selecting good seats in restaurants

If you eat out a lot, it is beneficial to know how to select the "best" tables in a restaurant. Never sit near washrooms, the kitchen, or the entrance to the restaurant. You don't want to be disturbed by unpleasant smells, busy waiters, or patrons going in and out of the restaurant. The best tables are those located diagonally opposite the restaurant entrance. Tables with window views are also considered good feng shui, as long as there is no glare from the outside. If you are reflected in one of the restaurant mirrors, it doubles the food on your table and is excellent. If you are out on an important date, try to sit facing your nien yen direction if you want the friendship to develop into a deeper relationship.

257 Activate the Southwest with boulders

Place a few large boulders with red double happiness symbols or red ribbon tied around them in the Southwest corner of your garden to enhance romance luck. The power of stones and boulders in an earth corner is like a catalyst for the matriarchal force to arise, benefiting not only the lady of the house, but also jumpstarting the marriage prospects of eligible sons and daughters living in the home who have reached marriageable age.

258 Cowrie shells help long distance romance

If you are in a long-distance relationship, place a fairly large conch or cowrie shell in the nien yen corner of your bedroom, or by your bedside to bring you and your lover more opportunities to be together. The cowrie shell adds luster to the relationship and helps it to have a happy ending. If you feel the distance that keeps you and your lover apart might be causing a cooling off in the relationship, send him or her a cowrie shell to create better bonding.

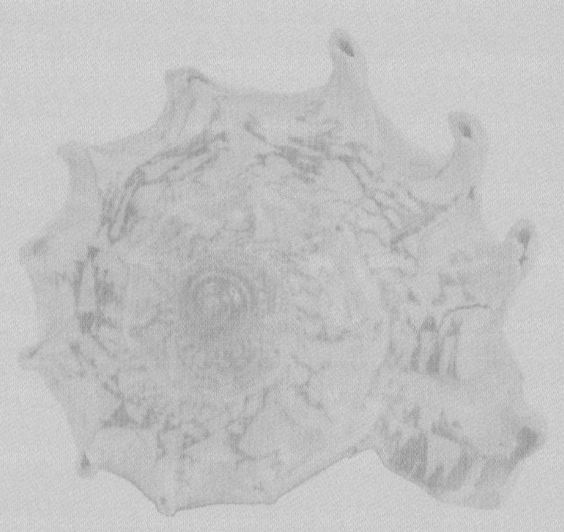

259 Boosting luck with windows

Windows that open outward are always luckier than windows that slide up and down. Outward-opening windows invite in the good fortune. If your windows slide up and down, then it is a good idea to frame your window with a darker colored paint—let outside chi be made aware that there is an opening through which it can enter the home. It is also a good idea to keep the window open as much as possible.

260 Beautiful peonies for a great son-in-law

If you have young single daughters, place peonies (or paintings of peonies) in the living room or on the landing of the staircase to bring them charming, eligible suitors with honorable intentions. A large painting of peonies in a home with plenty of daughters will attract excellent sons-in-law to the family. It creates happiness for the girls and for the parents as well.

261 Avoid peonies if you are in your fifties

Couples who have been married for a decade or more are advised not to place peonies in the bedroom, because they can cause the husband to pursue an affair with a younger woman. Peonies always suggest a young woman in full bloom—it is the king of flowers and its excellent effects benefit young couples. Those who are already middle-aged should definitely not have them hanging in the home, especially when all the children have already moved out to set up their own homes.

262 Avoid having a mirror directly facing your front door

A mirror that faces the front door causes all good fortune to flow out of the home. Whatever wealth or good fortune the family has simply cannot be retained. Money, position, and even relationships will slip through your fingers. If you must have a mirror in your foyer area, hang it on a wall that is not directly facing the door.

263 Jump start relationships with fire chi

Fire chi is especially great for jump-starting luck in the relationship areas of your life. The element of the relationship sector is Kun, or earth, which can be strengthened with fire chi. If you are not familiar with the formulas of feng shui and do not know how to find the best sectors to activate, simply consider the Southwest corners of your home, or rooms, to be the relationship luck areas. Remember that all the formulas complement each other and do not replace one another. Nor is there a ranking in potency and speed in seeing results.

264 Fire chi can also boost examination luck

Fire energy is also quite excellent for activating the chi of knowledge and wisdom. In the Pa Kua eight aspirations method we have identified the Northeast as the sector that can be activated for luck in acquiring knowledge. The element of the Northeast is earth and simply strengthening the Northeast corner of any room with fire energy (such as lamps or bright lights) will cause knowledge acquisition in the home to expand and accumulate. This brings excellent luck for those taking examinations.

Note that in the cycle of the elements, fire produces earth. Remember to place a dragon carp symbol in the Northeast corner to ensure good exam luck.

265 Guard your nien yen location

If there's a toilet, storeroom, or kitchen in your nien yen location in the house, you should not energize it, because it will lead to an unfulfilling and unlucky relationship. The location that corresponds to your nien yen location (based on the KUA formula) should also be checked for annual star afflictions. For instance, if your nien yen location is the South one year, then you must be aware that your love life will be afflicted by the Three Killings, which may be in the South that year. In the same way note that when the Five Yellow flies to the Northwest, then if this is your nien yen direction, your love life gets disturbed by the horrible Five Yellow.

266 Fire energy must never be too strong

A well-lit, cheerful bedroom is good for young, energetic couples, because it brings passionate yang energy into their love lives. However, this kind of fire energy should never be overdone. In feng shui, fire energy is a double-edged sword. It brings success, recognition, and imbues relationships and work with great passion. However, fire also has the potential to hurt when it is allowed to get too strong and hence out of control. At its worse, fire can burn and kill. So do not allow fire energy to get excessive. Note also that fire does not exist on its own, it is an element that has to be created. It also cannot be stored—but in feng shui its essence can be generated with light symbols. Use electrical lights to create a constant never-ending source of fire energy.

267 Avoid quarrelsome sectors when locating a marital bed

If you are a married couple, make sure that the bed you share is located in a sector with auspicious flying stars. Avoid particular sectors with the 2, 3 combination of flying stars. The way the flying stars are located throughout your house depends on its natal chart. To learn more about Flying Star feng shui and natal charts, refer to my book *Flying Star Feng Shui for Period 8*. Petty arguments between married couples are caused by the marital bed being in a corner of the bedroom afflicted by the quarrelsome star. If you cannot help it and there is nowhere else you can place your bed, use the colors red and gold to counter the quarrelsome energies of these troublesome stars.

268 Auspicious symbols enhance doors

Incorporate auspicious designs onto your main doors, because doing so will greatly enhance their potency in attracting good fortune into the home. Auspicious symbols that are excellent for attracting good luck are the mystical knot, the double fish, and the longevity symbol.

269 Solid doors are always better than glass doors

All the important doors of your home should be solid, and this includes the main door as well as the doors that lead into your bedroom. The doors define your living spaces and indicate solid protection for the residents. When the main door is weak, the home becomes vulnerable to all kinds of dangers and afflictions from surrounding negativities. Sliding or glass doors can be used as secondary doors.

270 Main door must be the largest

The main door into the home should always be the largest door. This ensures that the head of the family is properly respected and gets all the recognition that is due to him. When the main door is smaller than all other doors in the home, it implies that the family will get bullied and taken advantage of by others. It also means the father of the household cannot control his wife, nor his children.

271 Secondary doors should enhance the main door

If there are secondary entrance doors in other parts of the home, these must support the main door. Here is the checklist of proper positioning of secondary doors:

- If the main door is located in the North, it benefits from a secondary door in the West or in the Northwest.
- If the main door is located in the South, it benefits from a secondary door in the East or in the Southeast.
- If the main door is located in the West or Northwest, it benefits from a secondary door in the Southwest or in the Northeast.
- If the main door is located in the East or Southeast, it benefits from a secondary door in the North.
- If the main door is located in the Southwest or Northwest, it benefits from a secondary door in the South.

272 Bed sheet feng shui for a better sex life

Jazz up your sex life by swapping boring bed sheets and fluorescent lighting for sexy pink or red satin sheets and some candles or muted, romantic yellow lamps. The best way to introduce some zest into your love life is to use yellow or red lamps inside the bedroom. These create the right kind of yang energy. If you can find them, use red lanterns with the double happiness symbol written on them.

273 Carry a symbolic fan to ward off bad vibes

The fan has always been an effective shield against negative energy. It enables you to ward off any jealousy, envy, and anger that may be directed at you from people you do not know. Carrying a sandalwood fan is incredibly effective for protection, but you can also carry a symbolic gold-plated Monkey God fan. If you place something like this inside your purse, it protects you from being robbed.

274 Do not have a staircase facing the main door

When there is a staircase directly facing the front door, the chi that is entering the home becomes immediately afflicted. This is a feature that can cause grave misfortune for the family—even the loss of a family member. Staircases should always be kept a little away from the main door. To overcome this affliction, either move the staircase to end elsewhere, or use element cures. Thus:

• If the staircase is facing the door in a South direction, hang a faceted crystal between the staircase and the door.

• If the staircase is facing the door in a North direction, place a healthy plant between the staircase and the door.

• If the staircase is facing the door in a Southeast or East direction, hang a bright light between the staircase and the door.

• If the staircase is facing the door in a Southwest or Northeast direction, hang a six-rod metal wind chime between the staircase and the door.

• If the staircase is facing the door in a Northwest or West direction, place two urns of water between staircase and door.

275 Magic mirrors for protection

Single ladies who frequent nightspots should always carry a magic mirror in their purses for protection against unwanted attention and unpleasant situations. These mirrors are more powerful when they are made of brass with one side having a reflective surface and the other side having the longevity symbol and five bats pattern. The longevity sign protects against premature death and can be regarded as having talismanic powers.

276 Cover all exposed bookshelves

The killing energy created by the edges of shelves can cause friction between couples. In the office, they cause problems with employees and colleagues. Cover them with sliding doors. Even when the doors are made of glass, they can protect you from the unlucky knife-edge chi of the shelves. CEOs with exposed bookshelves behind them are certain to suffer from some health problems. Sometimes these book shelves can even cause you to lose your business, so it is wise to dismantle them or cover them.

277 Yin and yang in the bedroom

Make sure that you create the correct balance of yin and yang energies in your bedroom to make it easier to attract a partner. Yin vibrations are good for rest, but when yin is too strong, the lack of yang chi can result in a lonely love life. On the other hand, when yang chi is excessively strong, it can also represent obstacles to finding a suitable mate. Single women should never place a lone Dragon image inside the bedroom, as this is deemed to be too yang, causing them to have difficulty in their love life.

278 The Dragon and Phoenix enhance marriage prospects

For a happy marriage, and to improve your marriage prospects, display an image of the celestial pair—Dragon and Phoenix. When placed together as a pair, the Dragon and the Phoenix represent yang and yin respectively. The Dragon takes on the symbolism of the male yang essence, while the Phoenix takes on the female yin essence. This is one of the most powerful symbols of husband-and-wife chi energy, and when placed in your personalized love direction, or in the Southwest corner of the home, it creates marriage luck.

279 | Water features on your left please!

Always ensure that water features are placed on the left-hand side of the front door (when viewed from inside looking out) to avoid infidelity. No matter how auspicious it may be (under other formulas) to have water near your front door, if you inadvertently place it on the right-hand side of the door it causes the man of the house to develop a roving eye (at best) or to take on a second wife. So, if you do not want to lose your husbands, ladies, banish all water features from the right-hand side of your door. This applies to the inside and the outside of the house.

280 Love is a serious matter

You should only energize for love when you're ready for a serious relationship and commitment! Otherwise, you'll get more than you bargained for. Remember that in feng shui there is no such thing as a fling or a one-night stand. Love always means marriage and marriage always means starting a family. If you activate your love corner and you are not ready to settle down, you could be asking for trouble.

281 Crystal birds for togetherness luck

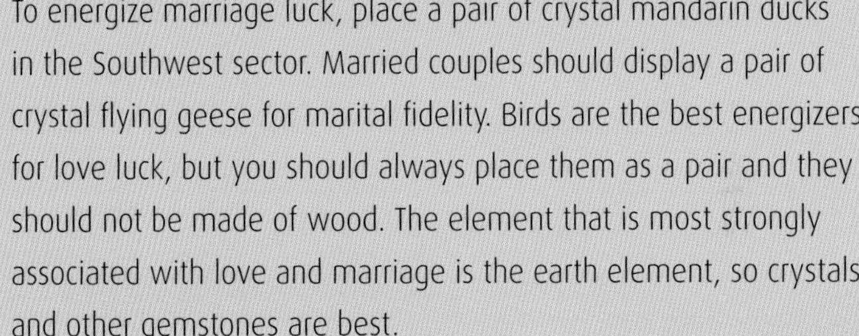

To energize marriage luck, place a pair of crystal mandarin ducks in the Southwest sector. Married couples should display a pair of crystal flying geese for marital fidelity. Birds are the best energizers for love luck, but you should always place them as a pair and they should not be made of wood. The element that is most strongly associated with love and marriage is the earth element, so crystals and other gemstones are best.

282 Keep the Southwest well lit at all times

Keep the flames of love alive by installing a bright light in the Southwest of your garden, living room, and even your bedroom. Lights signify fire energy and this produces earth, which is the symbolic element of mother energy. The mother trigram Kun signifies love, romance, and the nurturing care of family. Hence keeping the Southeast well lit at all times is excellent for love and family luck.

283 Hang curtains with love symbols

Hang curtains bearing symbols of love in your bedroom for marital bliss. Love symbols can be Western or Chinese, so flowers such as peonies and orchids can also be regarded as being love symbols. However, the most powerful symbol of love is the double happiness sign. This is said to attract the kind of energy that leads to domestic bliss and lots of happy occasions. Other love symbols are pictures of couples kissing and paired animals.

284 The personal love direction

The personal love direction is known as the nien yen direction. Always sit facing your nien yen when out on a date and always sleep with your head pointing to your nien yen to activate love luck while you are sleeping. The nien yen direction benefits each person individually. If you are already married and you and your spouse wish to conceive and start a family, but you are having a hard time, then sleeping with your heads pointed to the husband's nien yen direction will help. Remember the husband's direction is more important than the wife's direction.

285 Wear the double happiness symbol

Ignite romance luck by displaying a couple of red lanterns with the double happiness sign. Better yet, wear the double happiness symbol as fine jewelry, either as a ring on the ring finger of the left hand to attract a spouse, or wear it as earrings to prompt your current love to pop the question.

286 Red flowers can bring bad luck

Never send red flowers (long-stemmed red roses with thorns are the worst) to your love because this could well kill your romance. Never send red flowers to your wife or husband either. It signifies eventual separation and creates the cause for one party to find someone else. Also, do not include red flowers in a bouquet that is being sent to the hospital—red flowers usually mean "death" and this is not a good symbol to send to someone recovering in the hospital. Buddhists are also mindful never to place red flowers on their altar, because this is said to be most inauspicious.

287 How to marry into money

If you want to marry into money, try orienting your main door to face Northwest. This is supposed to be the direction that attracts matrimonial wealth luck. When the main door faces Northwest, it means the house is sitting Southeast and this is the wealth direction according to the Pa Kua symbolic method of energizing for eight aspirations. If you are staying with your parents and cannot change the main door, then find a room in the house that faces Northwest; then hang a large double happiness sign in the Southwest of the room. This will attract a rich suitor into your life. Note that feng shui cannot guarantee a good husband or wife—that is down to your own karma.

288 The mystical knot

Incorporate the mystical knot in your room décor to ensure an enduring happy marriage. This is a very powerful symbol that becomes even more potent during the period 8. The mystical knot brings all kinds of good fortune to your life, because it is really the number 8 and the infinity sign rolled into one. To create the mystical knot you need to "draw" the infinity sign three times. When you hang the knot in your car, rubbing it will help you find a parking space; and when you hang it on your purse, it protects your bag from being snatched. If you have ten purses, get ten of these knots tied with red string and carved out of jade. They have amazing potency.

289 | Moon magic visualization

For marriage luck, stimulate moon energy using a picture of scenery with the moon and moonlight. The Chinese have always believed that the god of marriage resides on the moon and this is why young maidens in search of husbands will benefit by sending thought messages to the god of marriage. On the fifteenth day of the month, when the moon is full, blow bubbles toward the moon and visualize your wishes contained inside the bubbles. Think of the bubbles being pink in color and visualize you and your spouse on your wedding day inside the pink bubble. This visualization has great potency, especially if you already have someone in mind.

290 Compatible KUA numbers

Generally, a partner in the same KUA group would be more compatible. So East group people should marry other East group people and those in the West group should marry those from the West group—this also makes it easier to feng shui your house, since you will have the same good directions. The following pairings of Ho Tu combinations of numbers are also auspicious:

- KUA 1 and 6 will enjoy wealth luck.
- KUA 2 and 7 will enjoy a very happy marriage.
- KUA 3 and 8 will enjoy excellent good fortune.
- KUA 4 and 9 will enjoy recognition and fame.

Couples with these above pairings of KUA numbers benefit if they can find a house with the number 5. This is because the 5 is the center number of the Ho Tu square.

291 Using the magic mirror when there is a full moon

A good way to use the magic mirror to make someone you are attracted to like you back, is to wait until you have a night with a full moon (you can check the lunar calendar or the Feng Shui Almanac for this); make sure that the day does not conflict with your animal year of birth; then prepare to imbue the mirror with the powerful energy of the moon. Your magic mirror should have auspicious etchings on the back—these can be the double happiness symbol, or the longevity symbol with five bats to symbolize five kinds of luck. Hold up the mirror so that both your face and the moon are reflected in the mirror. Make a silent wish. The next time you meet with the person you like, flash the mirror at him or her and you will see your magic mirror perform magic for you.

292 All interior doors should be of equal size

All the doors inside the house should be the same size. This does not include glass sliding doors, which are regarded as "openings." Doors here refer to solid wooden doors.

293 Choose your children's bedrooms according to their KUA

Rooms located in the East group directions are better for East group people, while West group directions are better for West group people. For couples who are married and sharing a room, if you and your spouse are from different groups, you should follow the husband's KUA. But for children who are in school, placing their bedroom so that it suits their KUA will make a big difference to how well they perform in exams, and how well they develop. East group children should try to stay in East, Southeast, South, or North rooms in the house. West group children should try to stay in Southwest, Northeast, Northwest, and West rooms. If you cannot achieve this for lack of rooms in the house, make sure that they sleep with their head pointed to a good direction for them.

294 All bedroom doors for children should be same size

When doors leading into children's bedrooms are different sizes, the occupant of the room with the larger door will come to dominate all the others. This is a good or bad thing depending on who occupies the room with the dominant door. Usually, I would place the eldest child inside the room with the largest door. Ideally however, I would prefer all the children of a household to grow up in equally with no single child dominating.

295 Keep your toilets and bathrooms small

In many of the old feng shui books, repeated warnings are given about the negative effect of toilets and bathrooms. In the old days, of course, toilets were always built a little away from the house and in the homes of the wealthy, toilets simply did not exist because chamber pots were used and these were taken out by servants. In modern homes, however, toilets are a real necessity, so the best solution is to keep the toilets in your home as small as possible. This reduces the effect of their negative chi.

296 Crystal apples bring peace to the home

The Chinese word for apple sounds like the word "peace" and as such, it is believed that having apples in the home create the cause for peace in the household. In the old days, apple trees were as highly desired as peach trees. In the current earth period, displaying crystal or glass apples in the home alongside crystal spheres will ensure harmony for the home. Quarrels are kept to a minimum and there are usually few misunderstandings.

297 Six crystal spheres for period 8 magic

One of the most powerful feng shui "features" to harness the earth chi of the period 8 combines the Taoist belief in the magic of smooth crystal spheres with the Pa Kua meaning of the number 6, which is "heaven chi." Thus, placing six crystal spheres in the center of the home, or in the center of the living room, is an excellent way of ensuring that life goes on smoothly with no major obstacles causing aggravation.

298 Activating the Northwest benefits the man of the house

It is very important to "protect" the Northwest sector of the home because this part of the house affects the luck of the patriarch—i.e., the man of the house. When the toilet of the house is located in the Northwest, it afflicts the luck of the husband, and if the Northwest corner is missing it can lead to some grave misfortune concerning him.

When single women live in a house or apartment with a missing Northwest corner, they will experience difficulty in finding husbands. You can simulate a Northwest corner by placing a bright light in the space where the Northwest corner would be.

299 Strengthen the Southwest to benefit the mother

While the Northwest benefits the father, it is the Southwest corner that affects the luck of the mother. You can strengthen this corner by placing earth element objects here. Some of the things you can do include painting the Southwest wall of the house an earth color, or hanging a map of the world, or placing a lighted crystal globe. Lights and crystals will always bring good fortune to the mother of the family when placed in the Southwest.

300 Activate the East for good health and family luck

The East sector governs the luck of the family and the longevity of family members. It ensures the family unit stays healthy, strong, and together. If you have elderly members of the family living with you, you should ensure your East sector is not afflicted. Ensure your toilet is not a prominent feature in the East. If you have a bathroom located in this sector of the house, keep the door closed at all times when not in use. Enhance for good health and longevity luck by using the elements of wood and water for the décor of this sector. The colors blue and green are suitable in this sector. You should also keep this part of the home active. Do not let the chi here get stale. If you don't spend enough time in this part of the home, keep a radio there and let it play for at least three hours a day.

301 Activate the West for descendant luck

If you want good children, or when you simply want children and are having a hard time conceiving, what you should do is to activate the West location of your living room, or your bedroom. Do this by placing "children images" in the West and then activating these images with lights. I suggest placing the five colors of the lava lamp because these lamps serve an excellent feng shui function. The lights signify fire energy, while the moving oil inside the lamp signifies water energy. The different colors of the lamps represent the other elements. By turning the lamps on for at least three hours a day, the West corner (which stands for descendants) will have strong energy, benefiting the children of the house and causing children to be born to the household.

302 Activate the Northeast for education luck

The Northeast is the sector that brings luck to students and scholars. Children who are still studying will benefit from a Northeast that is well enhanced. Since the Northeast is represented by earth energy, use crystals and images of globes in this sector to bring out the good energy of this sector. Make sure it is not afflicted by a toilet or kitchen. If it is, do not enhance the sector, and instead enhance the small chi of your children's study room and the small chi of the living room by placing crystals in the Northeast corners of these individual rooms. The Northeast also brings luck to anyone who is involved in research, communication, journalism, and the creative arts.

303 Enhance the South if you want recognition

If you find yourself working like a dog, but never getting the recognition you deserve from your boss, you need to start activating the South. The South is the sector that governs everything to do with how others perceive you. You will find that no matter how good you are, if you have an afflicted South, you will be under-appreciated and your efforts and talents will go unrecognized. Do not let this happen. Make sure the South sector of your home or living room is always brightly lit, active, and vibrant. Use the color red or green to enhance the fire energy of the sector, or use a painting of a hundred birds. This is also a good corner to display your tribute or victory horses.

304 Always remember your directions in meetings

If you are in an important meeting where you want things to go your way, if you are negotiating something, or if you are trying to convince the other party of something, make sure you are sitting in one of your auspicious directions according to your KUA. Of course, you should also make sure your work desk is facing your sheng chi (success direction), but sitting the right way during meetings is just as important. Taking this extra step when you plan your meetings can make all the difference, especially if your work involves sales, negotiations, and deal-making. All you need to do is carry a small pocket compass, and nowadays you can get them on key chains, watches, and wallets, so they are not a hassle to carry around.

305 Boardroom feng shui

If you are director of a company or your job requires you to attend meetings frequently, here are some sitting tips:

- Sit furthest away from the door. Diagonally opposite the door is the best direction.
- Sit with a solid wall behind you for support.
- Never sit with a window behind you, especially if the meeting is held high up in a multilevel building.
- Do not sit anywhere where your feet point to the door because this is considered a bad position.
- Never, ever sit with your back to the door, because you will constantly worry about people behind you.
- Avoid being "hit" by exposed overhead beams and sharp protruding corners.

306 When interviewing for a job

Interview feng shui requires you to sit facing one of your good directions. You need not face your best direction—in fact, the fu wei direction is the better direction to activate good luck at interviews. Inside your pocket you should have a small single-point crystal or a jade hanging depicting the five rats. This will enable you to land the job you want more easily. Here is your fu wei direction based on your KUA number.

1	North
2	SW
3	East
4	SE
5	*
6	NW
7	West
8	NE
9	South

* SW for men and NE for women.

307 Creating auspicious examination luck

For examination luck, you should definitely sit facing your fu wei direction and in your pocket you should have a small jade image of a carp poised to jump the dragon gate. Indeed, if those of you still in school or at college display a beautiful crystal or gemstone carp shown poised to jump the dragon gate, it will bring you loads of good examination luck. The dragon gate legend tells of the humble carp swimming upriver and jumping across the gate to become a dragon. For as long as anyone can remember, this has been a metaphor for passing the imperial examinations, which in the old days were the passport to "fame and glory" at the emperor's court.

308 Feng shui travel cures

If you have no choice but to make an important journey from an inauspicious direction, you can minimize the harmful effects of this by taking a detour. For a major move, it is recommended that you stay at least six weeks in your in-between stop to weaken the negative influences of the first part of the journey. Since this solution is often difficult, here is a list of things you can do to dilute inauspicious chi when traveling from your unlucky directions.

- If traveling from the East or Southeast, use a curved metal knife to swipe the air in front of you before you start your journey.
- If traveling from the South, sprinkle several drops of water in front of you three times before you start your journey.
- If traveling from the North, take some earth from your garden and throw it in the space in front of you before starting your journey.
- If traveling from the West or Northwest, light three candles and swipe the air three times with the candles before your journey.
- If traveling from the Southwest or Northeast, look for a spray of pine needles and swipe the air three times before your journey.

309 When relocating, check your directions

The same rules apply for when you plan to relocate. If you are being transferred, see if the move is good for you, by checking the direction you are coming from. If it is one of your good directions, it will be good. If not, it will bring misfortune unless you undertake some remedies.

310 Choose the correct destination for overseas study

Those of you who are contemplating an overseas education, do take note that you must select your destination correctly. Generally, according to the KUA formula, you should ensure that you travel from a good direction. So you must travel from a direction that brings you luck. This usually means that West group people (KUA numbers 2, 5, 6, 7, and 8) should travel to colleges from the West, Northwest, or Southwest. Then they will do well and attain great honors. Those who belong to the East group (KUA numbers 1, 3, 4, and 9) should travel from the East, Southeast, North, or South.

311 Activating your animal sign location

One easy way of improving your personal feng shui is to activate and enhance the space in your home that corresponds to your animal sign direction. Every animal sign in the Chinese Zodiac has an associated compass location. To find your animal sign, you will need to check your date of birth, and to find out your direction—refer to the compass graphic shown below. To activate the direction, simply place a symbol of your animal sign in the corresponding direction.

312 Energizing the four important trigrams

There are four important trigram locations in each home and these refer to the four people in the traditional family unit: the father (trigram Chien), the mother (trigram Kun), the son (trigram Ken), and the daughter (trigram Sun). Activating these trigrams means making certain that the four secondary directions of the patriarch, the matriarch, the sons, and the daughters of the family are not afflicted or missing, and are properly energized.

313 Trigrams that benefit the children

To activate the children corners, boost the Northeast (Ken trigram) and the Southeast (Sun trigram) corners of the house. If they are missing, activate the equivalent corners in the living or dining rooms. The Northeast benefits the sons and also signifies education luck and examinations. To activate it, use fire energy. The Southeast benefits the daughters of the family. It is also the wealth corner. To activate it, use plenty of lush healthy growing plants.

314 Activating trigram Kun for family happiness

When you activate the Southwest, the place of the Kun trigram, you will not only benefit the mother, but will also generate the luck of relationships for the whole family. When the mother is lucky, everyone benefits. The best method of doing this is to use fire energy, so place bright crystal lights in the Southwest.

315 Energizing trigram Chien to benefit the father

The first trigram to activate is Chien, which is the Northwest direction. This part of the house must be energized to benefit the patriarch. Irrespective of whether this direction is favorable or not for the man of the house, you should still activate the Northwest. Since the element here is metal, it benefits from earth energy, so placing a large crystal in the Northwest brings excellent feng shui for the patriarch, which in turn ensures protection for the family.

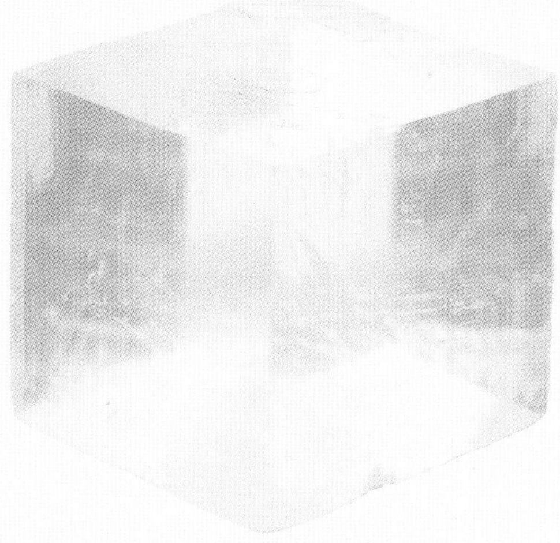

316 Is your apartment building lucky for you?

To check if your apartment is lucky for you, check whether the building has affinity with your KUA number. To find out, use a compass to check the facing and sitting direction of the apartment building. Now see if these two directions are lucky for you based on your KUA number.

If your KUA number is 1, 3, 4, or 9, you belong to the East group and all East directions (East, Southeast, North, and South) will be auspicious for you. So if the building is facing or sitting any of these directions, the apartment building is good for you. Remember to take the facing direction first, and then the opposite of the facing is the sitting direction.

If your KUA number is 2, 5, 6, 7, or 8, you belong to the West group and your lucky directions are West, Northwest, Northeast, and Southwest.

317 Activating with good fortune symbols

You can practice feng shui by simply placing the traditional auspicious symbols within the home. For instance, you will rarely find Chinese homes without the three star gods known as the Fuk Luk Sau. These three Taoist deities symbolize health, wealth, and longevity for households that have their presence in the home.

Other important symbols that bring good fortune include the Dragon-Tortoise, the three-legged toad, the four celestial guardians (dragon, phoenix, tortoise, and tiger), and the important symbols of the five bats (for abundance), the money tree (gem tree), which brings accumulation of wealth, as well as plenty of coins, ingots, and precious stones. When these auspicious symbols of prosperity are present in the home, they signify abundance, making it easy for good fortune chi to flow in.

318 The pumpkin is great for energizing abundance luck

The pumpkin, though not as famous as the three-legged toad and sailing ship as a wealth enhancer, brings wealth of a different kind to the household. This vegetable is symbolic of great prosperity in abundance, of always having enough to eat, and of the wealth to carry on for generations to come. It is also a symbol of fertility, which brings the promise of generations of children and grandchildren to carry on the family name. It is best displayed in the Southeast for wealth, but placing a jeweled pumpkin anywhere in the home will attract good fortune.

319 The Ru Yi brings authority luck for parents with naughty kids

The Ru Yi is more well known as an instrument for bosses to control their subordinates, for leaders to control their subjects, and for people in high positions to keep their rank and post. It is known also as the scepter of office. However, it is also very useful in the home to control wayward children. Displayed in the Northwest, it increases the moral authority of the father in the house. It is no use trying to control modern kids with force; you need them to respect and to listen to you. By calling on the powers of the Ru Yi, you strengthen the patriarch and thereby the harmony of the whole family. To improve influence of the mother, place the Ru Yi in the Southwest.

320 The famous three-legged toad

Another powerful symbol that is believed to attract wealth luck into the home is the popular three-legged toad. It is best when this image is carved from a single piece of rock crystal or other precious gemstone. The current period 8 is the earth period so that when an auspicious image is carved out of a treasure of the earth, such as crystal, citrine, or amethyst, it becomes doubly energizing. Three-legged toads made of brass or plaster are also excellent when placed in the living room, under sofas and tables. Do not place this symbol on your altar or high up on cupboards. They are best when placed on the floor and looking at the door. A good number of toads to have in the home is nine.

321 Hang faceted crystals to bring in the good chi

One of the best ways of inviting in the good fortune yang energy of the cosmos is by hanging faceted crystals in your windows. This brings in the essence of the sunshine, which contains powerful light energy. The crystal facets usually break the light into the seven colors of the rainbow—these awaken the seven chakras of the human body and align them with the seven planets that bring good cleansing energy. The best is to try and invite in the early morning sunshine, so make sure you have crystals hanging from your East windows.

322 The six-tier waterfall

Build a six-tier waterfall in your garden to attract good fortune from heaven. A six-tier waterfall is a perfect manifestation of tien ti ren (heaven, earth, and humankind) energy, bringing wealth, harmony, and happiness to households. The water in such man-made waterfalls should be kept clean, so there should be a filter. The water should fall into a small pond in which you can keep fish. Make sure the pond is deep enough for your fish to be safe from predators such as birds and rats. Place such a waterfall in the North, East, or Southeast, and in this period 8 having water in the Southwest is said to be extremely auspicious. Wherever you have this water feature, make sure there is an opening into the home—either a door or a window so that the good chi created is able to enter into the home.

323 Finding the place for prosperity water

There are different ways of finding the correct spot for placing prosperity water, but probably the best method is to use the Flying Star method, which uses relevant house natal charts to identify the place of the auspicious water stars. This method of feng shui is based on the facing directions of houses from which a road map of auspicious sectors can be identified. A good tip is thus for you to familiarize yourself with Flying Star feng shui. In the meanwhile, if you place a small water feature in the North or in the Southwest, you will not go wrong. Identify the North or Southwest corner of your home using a proper compass.

324 Foyers should be well lit

Make certain that the small area just inside your house or office is always kept well lit. This is good feng shui practice. Even at night, it is a good idea to keep at least one light turned on in the foyer. This ensures that the chi of your home never has a chance to become excessively yin during the night-time hours.

325 Use of colors for enhancement

There are two principles that govern the use of colors in feng shui—the theory of the five elements and the theory of yin and yang. Colors are very effective irrespective of which feng shui method you are using. Colors refer to the rainbow colors, while their yin or yang aspects depend on their intensity and their shade. As a general rule, the darker the color, the more yin it is, because of the greater preponderance of black. By the same token, the lighter the shade, the more yang the color is said to be, due to the presence of white. Black is a yin color, while white is a yang color. Having said that, please do note that red is considered a yang color. Similarly, yellow is also a yang color. In fact, these two colors symbolize good fortune manifesting vibrant yang energy. Colors in feng shui can be used according to the location of the sector being decorated. Another approach is based on an individual's KUA number, from which it is possible to identify the color that can enhance that person's feng shui.

326 Reds in the South bring upward mobility

The color red is associated with the South. It belongs to the fire element in the theory of the five elements and when it is present in the South, the color Red brings recognition, success, and promotion luck. Red in the South of the house, or the South of the living room or dining room, brings vibrant yang energy. Take note however that the most auspicious red colors are cinnabar red, new year red, and ox blood red.

327 Special properties of red and gold

Fabulous recognition luck is always created by the auspicious combination of red and gold. Gold creates wealth luck while red becomes the activating medium. Thus when you place coins tied with red string in any location, they attract wealth luck. For this reason, those who know always place hundreds of three coins tied with red string embedded under their floors and in their walls when building their homes. This creates the aura of wealth luck around the home. The meaning of red and gold together also signifies high office, happy occasions, and prosperity luck. The auspicious attributes of this color combination make them a great favorite during the lunar new year. However, as with all feng shui symbols that possess so much potency, it is vital never to overdo it. Red and gold, for instance, should not be used inside the bedroom.

328 Prosperity power of purple

There is a Chinese saying that goes something like "things are going so well that even red becomes purple." The implication is that purple is a very powerful color and while it does not enjoy the same royal reverence that it enjoys in the West, purple is nevertheless regarded as a very prosperous color. To activate purple, use it only as a feature wall. For this purpose the wall that benefits most from purple is the North wall, because here it signifies water, which means prosperity. When you paint the North wall purple, you are activating its yin side. When you paint the South wall purple, you are activating its yang side—and both these dimensions of purple are auspicious. So the choice is yours.

329 Silver and purple spells money

The combination of silver with purple has been my signature color combination through many successful business deals. This is because the words silver and purple sounds like "ngan chee" in Cantonese, which means "money." So the combination of purple with silver has very powerful and positive connotations for wealth luck. In terms of the elements, this combination also suggests the water element that dominates, because water is produced by metal.

330 Green and blue brings growth

Blue and green together is both harmonious and well balanced and in terms of meanings this combination attracts growth energy. Paintings of mountains done in green and blue are especially auspicious when hung in the East or Southeast of your home. They ensure that there will be expansion of family wealth as well as rise to prominence of the sons of the family.

331 Yellow and white for power

This combination contains the attributes of power as signified by the strength of the metal element. Here, the earth element of yellow produces the white of metal. At the same time, yellow is considered an imperial color which, when combined with white, suggests the presence of gold. Sometimes, such a combination may be too yang, too auspicious for some people. If you feel uncomfortable with this combination of colors, especially when painted in your home, make the yellow a lot lighter in color. Yellow energy always brings success, but you may not be able to sustain the heavy chi of yellow—the indication of this being the case is if you fall ill. If you cannot take this imperial color, change back to white. For those of you who have the inner chi to benefit from the combination, enhance it further by displaying something made of gold in your living room.

332 Green and red for fame and recognition

This color combination always suggests Christmas to the Westerner, but to the Chinese feng shui expert, green and red are the best color combination for generating the luck of fame, popularity, and recognition. This is a combination that spells success. Green strengthens red when based on the productive cycle of the five elements. Wood makes fire big and powerful. So to bring good fortune to the family and especially success that benefits the sons of the family, use this combination in their rooms after they have passed the age of twelve.

333 Red and yellow in earth corners

These two colors can be pretty awesome in terms of the luck they generate. When used correctly (i.e., placed in the earth sectors of the Southwest, the Northeast, or the center of the house), and for people who have affinity with these colors, they will immediately experience a surge of good fortune. New projects come by, they receive a windfall of money, or something they have been eyeing suddenly drops into their lap. But to some, however, once again this color scheme may be deemed too "heavy." It is advisable to be careful. If you benefit from this color combination, stick to it as it will bring you good fortune. But if you feel uncomfortable (e.g., if you get angry, or feel aggravated and uncomfortable) these are signs that the combination is not for you.

334 Black and white for yin and yang

This is an awesome combination because it symbolizes the tai chi of yin and yang. Black signifies water, which is produced by white metal so the combination is balanced and harmonious. This combination augurs well for sectors that benefit from the water element. Water is usually activated for the purpose of generating wealth luck so the black and white tai chi symbol is a very good catalyst.

335 Black and green for abundance

This combination brings similar effects as blue and green. Water produces wood, so this color combination is excellent for the wood sectors of East and Southeast. If your home is predominantly painted in a combination of these two colors, it will benefit the children, both sons and daughters. Since wood always signifies growth chi, it suggests expansion and increase.

336 Yang colors for corridors

The corridors of your home are important passageways for chi to move from room to room. Corridors channel the flow of energy within the living space so the feng shui of these spaces is extremely important. Corridors benefit from bright yang colors such as white, as this facilitates the movement of chi. When corridors are too narrow or too long and straight, the result is often very fast-moving chi, which can be harmful to residents. You can then use different colors to slow down the chi.

337 Activating for good feng shui room by room

A great way to practice feng shui is to do it on a room-by-room basis. We all know that some rooms are more important than others, such as our own bedroom, as well as the room where we spend the most amount of time. Identify the room that is the most important to you and then look on it as your personal tai chi space.

Next, use a compass to identify the different corners of the room that symbolize your most important aspirations. For instance, the Southwest corner will signify your love aspirations and the North will be your career aspirations corner. This uses the eight aspirations method. You can also superimpose other types of feng shui charts and activate the corners systematically so that the whole room becomes energized to fulfill all your goals and dreams. Now do the same for other rooms within the home.

338 Update your feng shui each year

It is also vitally important to remember that feng shui has a time dimension, so you must update your feng shui cures and remedies as well as your energizers and activators regularly. There are annual as well as monthly updates, so you should be alert to the changes in chi energy in your space. The most efficient way to keep track is to use the annual feng shui chart contained in the yearly WOFS Almanac calendar, and to use the monthly updates that are analyzed in the *Feng Shui World* bi-monthly magazines. You should look out for them when they get released each time, because they do tend to sell out within the first week of release. Or you can obtain regular updates from the www.wofs.com website.

Once you are aware of where the different afflictions are located, and you know what remedies to put in place, protecting your home or office becomes a very easy thing to do.

339 The feng shui chart

Look out for the annual feng shui charts and their explanations each year at the start of the new year.

In this example for the year of the Wood Rooster, the ruling Lo Shu number is 4 so this will be a year when love and relationships take center stage. It is also a year when older women tend to exert a greater influence over how things get done. The year of the Wood Rooster is the year of the bird. Displaying birds in the South or near entrances into the home will be most auspicious. The bird brings opportunities and dissolves gossip and troublemaking vibrations effectively.

	SE	SOUTH	SW	
	3 HOSTILE	8 GOOD	1 GOOD	
E	3 KILLINGS 2 ILLNESS	4 LOVE	GD JUPITER 6 GOOD	W
	7 VIOLENCE	9	5 MISFORTUNE	
	NE	NORTH	NW	

Note that in this example, the East and Southeast are quite severely afflicted with the illness and hostile stars respectively. The Five Yellow meanwhile has flown to the Northwest.

340 Five-element pagodas keep misfortunes away

In addition to the twenty-year period chi, there is also the phenomena of annual and monthly chi changes that affect our well being, our luck, and even our frame of mind. The principle of feng shui is that energy is constantly moving and changing so a large part of feng shui practice is focused on knowing how these changes in chi affect us, as well as how to locate pockets of afflictions around the home. One of the major causes of misfortune is the influence of the Five Yellow, which is the name given to the number 5 in the Flying Star chart. When the Five Yellow flies into your bedroom, it brings misfortunes, anger, accidents, and a great deal of stress. It must be kept under control by the five-element pagoda made of brass or gold plated over steel. The metal energy is a vital part of the remedy. Sometimes, one small pagoda is insufficient to overcome this misfortune star, especially when the house is big and the center of the home is spacious and open.

341 Remedies to defeat the illness star

Always use the six-rod, all-metal wind chime to defeat the illness-bringing number 2 star. If you sleep in a room located in the corner of your house occupied by the illness star, you will surely succumb to illness unless you hang the metal wind chime here. This is a powerful cure. In addition, try also to sleep with head pointed to your personal tien yi direction (based on your KUA number). If your room is located in the illness star corner, using these two remedies will help all residents residing within to overcome the illness chi here. The chart showing the tien yi directions for each of the nine KUA numbers is shown here:

1	East
2	West
3	North
4	South
5	*
6	NE
7	SW
8	NW
9	SE

* West for men and NW for women.

342 | Clear clutter at least once a week

Set aside some time one day every week to be your decluttering time. It is incredible how quickly clutter can build up if you don't clean it out on a regular basis. This includes all kinds of clutter. Clutter you haven't had the time to clear out, clutter you keep for sentimental reasons, and clutter that happens because you are basically a messy person. Be ruthless about your clearing. Don't turn your clutter-clearing session into a reminiscing session. If you let yourself get side-tracked every time you try and declutter, you will never get the job done. Start simple, with just the tabletop, eventually moving on to reorganizing your drawers, cabinets, and cupboards. You will even find the exercise of decluttering therapeutic.

343 Transforming into period 8 chi

In feng shui, time is divided into nine periods of twenty years with each period being ruled by an element and a number. We are currently in the period that is ruled by the element of earth and the number 8—hence this is known as the period 8. It began on February 4th, 2004 and will last until February 4th, 2024. All homes and buildings will benefit from having their chi revitalized, thereby transforming it into period 8 chi. This ensures that within their homes and buildings, the chi energy continues to stay vigorous and healthy. Transforming into period 8 chi requires knowledge of Flying Star feng shui. This introduces the concept of time influences in feng shui.

344 Red Laughing Buddha dissolves anger

The hostile and quarrelsome star brought by the number 3 almost always causes anger in the home or office. This is a wood element star and it brings very aggravating effects, causing quarrels leading to violence or court cases. Legal entanglements often start when the number 3 star flies into your bedroom, or to the center of the home, or worse, when it flies into the sitting palace of the home. When the house is facing one direction, the opposite of that is the sitting direction, and when the 3 flies into this sitting direction it is said to be occupying the sitting palace of the home. Residents will become angry, upset, and quick-tempered. To dissolve this anger, the best remedy is to use a Laughing Buddha dressed in red robes and carrying an ingot. If this cure is unsuitable for you, try using red colored pillow cases, paintings, or carpets placed next to a sword made of coins tied with red string. Generally, having a small red robed Laughing Buddha on your office desk goes a long way towards dispelling anger directed at you.

345 Cleaning leftover chi from previous tenants

This kind of chi must absolutely be "cleansed" before you move in. Before renting any home, it is a good idea to enquire about the previous tenants. Negative chi lingers in homes formerly occupied by people who were ill, especially if the sickness was terminal or of the mental kind. Walls, floors, and ceilings retain left behind attitudes, anger, pain, tension, and unhappiness that must be cleared before new energy can flow smoothly in.

The best way to cut through such negative energy is by using the power of metal sounds. Thus bells, cymbals, and best of all singing bowls are excellent for "cutting through" negative energies. Invest in a singing bowl that is made from seven different types of metal and then learn to make the bowl "sing." Walking around rooms in the house with the singing bowl singing three times in a clockwise direction will lift the chi of the home, in the process transforming negative energy into crisp new positive energy.

346 When illness strikes, use metal chi

When residents succumb to illness, it is almost always due to the intangible afflictions brought by illness stars into parts of the home that make up the facing palace (i.e., the foyer areas where the main door is located) or into the bedroom. Illness stars are part of the Flying Star method of feng shui and their impact on the health luck of residents can be very severe.

Overcome these illness stars with strong metal energy—hang metal six-rod wind chimes in the bedroom of the sick person. Even if you are not certain exactly where the illness star may be, hanging a metal wind chime protects against illness chi.

347 Living near hospitals and cemeteries

The danger of living too close to buildings such as hospitals and police stations or being too close to a cemetery is the close proximity to yin spirits. These are places where yin spirit formation builds up on a regular basis and if you are too close, you will feel your energy sapping away, making you more vulnerable to illness and misfortune. Use fire energy in the form of incense burning and bright lights to overcome the build-up of excessive yin chi. Keep your home well lit at all times and if necessary, you can also consider painting the wall facing the hospital or cemetery a bright red.

348 Potent purifiers from the high mountains

Go shopping for the precious herbal incense made from the plants that grow in the high mountains. Mine comes from the Himalayan region of Solu Khumbu, which lies on the Kathmandu side of the mountain range. Here the mountain herbs and shrubs grow sparingly, because it is cold up there at about 11,000 feet above sea level. But it is not too cold for the plants to grow. The energy is strong and pure and when burned as incense, it is amazingly efficient at cleansing the space. It also gives off a distinctive pungent aroma that is very purifying.

349 The sacred incense cure

In recent years, aromatherapy has become very popular because the Western world has at last woken up to the power of aromas. In the East, we have always used the power of incense to keep our homes cleansed of evil spirits and bad chi. In fact, there are many incense cures that can be used as purification rituals. One of the simplest is to look for your favorite incense—mine are sandalwood incenses as well as herbal incense from the high mountains—and then place it on a red glowing piece of charcoal held on a plate. Walk around your rooms three times in a clockwise direction and as you watch the incense smoke spiraling upward, imagine that it absorbs all negative chi, leaving the room crisp and filled with clean energy.

350 Sound therapy for your space

Sound therapy inside the home is created by the use of wind chimes, bells, bamboos, and other natural sounds. The sound of flowing water is one of the most yang-creating sounds that attracts vibrant fresh chi into homes. Sound therapy brings precious yang chi into the space and if you wish, you can also play music through the day to create happy chi. Make an effort never to leave the home silent for too long. When you go on holidays, keep the radio turned on as this is the best way to keep the chi flowing and the yang energy presence maintained.

351 Crystal spheres to ease tensions

An excellent way to dissolve tension in the home is to arrange six crystal and glass spheres in the family areas of the home. Where there is a great deal of fighting, quarreling, shouting, and anger, smooth crystal spheres will calm the situation and absorb all the angst and tension that hangs in the air. The crystal spheres (also known as crystal balls) will encourage smoothness in relationships between siblings and spouses. The number 6 is significant because it represents heaven luck, which combines effectively with the earth element of the crystal.

352 When all your relationships seem to go wrong

When things start going wrong for you in your interactions with people—loved ones, colleagues, and associates—you can suspect that you may be manifesting a vulnerability to the intangible bad chi brought by changing Flying Stars. If you do not know anything about this powerful branch of feng shui, simply try hanging a pagoda wind chime near your front door and one inside your bedroom by the side of a wall. When aggravating Flying Stars cause relationship problems, you can improve the situation by hanging wind chimes. If this does not resolve the situation, you might have too many plants in the Southwest corners of your house, of your living room or dining room. If so, thin out wood energy, as this could be causing havoc in your social life.

353 Yin water cure to dissolve anger

The yin water cure is an excellent antidote to continuous anger, which leads to violence. Water has the power to cool down the atmosphere of anger very effectively, especially when it is yin or quiet water. When quarrels take place between spouses or lovers, the yin water can be empowered with moon energy. Place an urn of water in your garden or on your apartment balcony on a night of the full moon and allow the water to absorb the energy of the moon. Then bring the water inside the home. Pour it into vases and beautiful containers, which become effective keepers of the peace. Remember, phonetically, "vases" sounds like "peace" in Chinese and are very highly regarded in feng shui as one of the eight auspicious objects.

354 Colored crystal balls will calm you

Displaying crystal balls in a variety of colors is an effective cure against harmful gossip and slander. Place a combination of six smooth crystal balls—in white or pink—to calm troubled nerves. Green crystal ball spheres will silence all gossip about your business and expansion plans, while blues heal and lavender awakens an inner calm. When you display these wonderful treasures of the earth, you will discover that fewer things faze you than before. Remember, the effect of crystal spheres is usually very calming.

355 | Overcoming legal entanglements

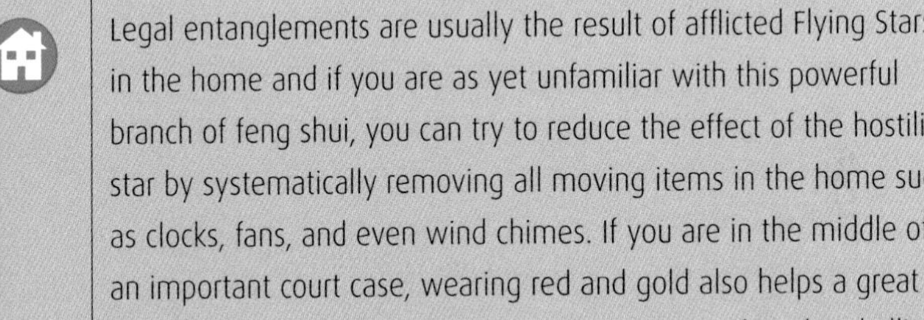

Legal entanglements are usually the result of afflicted Flying Stars in the home and if you are as yet unfamiliar with this powerful branch of feng shui, you can try to reduce the effect of the hostility star by systematically removing all moving items in the home such as clocks, fans, and even wind chimes. If you are in the middle of an important court case, wearing red and gold also helps a great deal. Carry the astrological amulets of your secret friend and allies based on the astrology of the twelve animals.

356 Coin swords banish jealousy vibes

You could well become a victim of some silly jealous competitor, a spurned admirer, or an envious colleague. Here, people who are against you are simply jealous. Nevertheless, they can be dangerous, so it is a good idea to arm yourself with protection. In feng shui, the concept of protection is very popular and many people wear more than a single item with talismanic properties. As an interim measure however, always use a sword made of coins tied with red string. Place it in the center of the home—a place that does not get in the way of the flow of chi.

357 Space cleansing after a burglary

If your house has just been burgled, or if you have just had your car robbed, you could be suffering from Flying Star afflictions that bring this about. To cleanse the after-effects of such a frightful experience, use a mixture of saffron and salt water to cleanse the doorways and windows of your home. All the openings into the home should get the once over with this mixture so that not even a single trace of the frightful energy is allowed to linger. To guard against being robbed a second time, place a pair of Chi Lins high above your gate or front door. Always place the Chi Lin facing out with the female Chi Lin (the one with a baby) on the right-hand side of the house (as viewed from inside facing out). Another great tip I picked up a long time ago was to place an inverted broomstick by the main door. This is said to ward against robbery. A final cure is the rhinoceros. Placed inside the house within the vicinity of the door, this is an effective cure.

358 Creating peach blossom luck in the bedroom

Activate the four powerful purveyors of peach blossom luck in your bedroom by placing a Rooster in the West of your bedroom, a Horse in the South, a Rabbit in the East, and a Rat in the North. This ensures total fidelity luck.

359 Cleansing the sleeping space

If you find it hard to sleep night after night, you should undertake a thorough investigation of the bedroom. Get rid of unused nails on walls, paintings of wild animals, and waterfall images that send fierce water toward the sleeping couple. There are three simple rituals you can try to improve the sleeping space:

• Place an amethyst geode under your feet, under the bed. Tie it to the bedpost with red string. This also ensures fidelity in the marriage.

• For extra cleansing, place your pillows and mattress in the bright sunshine to absorb the yang chi of bright sunlight. Place your pillows in the sun for at least three hours.

• Once a month, light fragrant incense and walk clockwise around the room. Do this for three rounds and you will efficiently remove all lingering negative chi from your sleeping space. You can use any kind of incense you wish.

360 Mirror ritual to bring back a loved one

We call this the mirror spell. You need a picture of your lover. Pictures used in this ritual should be full body and ideally should have been taken outdoors. If only the face is visible, the picture has been cropped and is unsuitable. Next, take a corresponding picture of yourself, preferably a picture that shows you smiling. Now taking two mirrors, stick the picture of yourself on the back of one mirror and a picture of your lover on the back of the other.

Next place the mirrors together so that the two pictures face each other. Now tape the mirrors together and keep them safe until the next full moon. Bring the mirrors out and shine them at the moon. This is the most important part of the ritual because it invokes the help of the god of marriage who resides on the moon. Keep the sandwiched pictures and two mirrors until you recover your lover. As soon as everything is back to normal, release the pictures!

361 A fire ritual to dissolve blockages

Here is a fire ritual to dejunk the mind of old grudges, hurts, and anger. Simply write down anything and everything that ever made you angry, disgusted, or frustrated. List names of people you know who may have offended or snubbed you. Next, think of the events and situations of confrontations you may have had with anyone. Spend time making the list of complaints you have against the world. When you are sure there is nothing left, put all the pieces of paper together and symbolically burn all your emotional baggage. Let go of old hurts and past disappointments. You will discover that performing this simple fire ritual will make your life brighter and you will be ready to take on new challenges.

362 A grounding ritual at the hour of the Dragon

There is an amazing Taoist ritual that enables you to draw energy from deep within the earth to revitalize the chi of your home when you feel that its chi has slackened. Think of your house as having a thick grounding cord like a tubular root connecting it to the very center of the earth, soaking the deep energy of the earth and bringing it into the home. Do this visualization at the hour of the Dragon, i.e., between 7:am and 9:am. This exercise brings powerful empowerment to the home. The effect is that residents feel lighter and more energized.

363 Three sure ways to avoid splitting up with your partner

To ensure that you and your spouse do not split up, here are three tips that you must observe:

• Never allow reflective surfaces to face the bed. We have seen how harmful mirrors can be. So if you have mirrors in your bedroom, dismantle them.

• Never have water inside the bedroom. Here I am referring to water such as aquariums, not a glass of water.

• Never allow two separate mattresses on a single king or queen size bed. When a married couple sleep is when they bond closer.

364 Borrowing the chi of holy places

If you visit holy places as well as places of pilgrimage, you can "borrow" the chi of these holy places by taking a little bit of the earth from the ground and then, when you bring the earth back to your home, sprinkling it in your garden. This way, the holy chi instantly takes root in your garden. My garden contains the holy chi of many pilgrimage places—perhaps that is why my flowers bloom so big and so frequently, and maybe also why my plants grow so strong and healthy.

365 Creating a protective forcefield

You can use your mind to create a blue cocoon of light around you for protection. To do this visualization correctly, all you need is to train your mind to concentrate on a sphere of blue light just above your head, as if it had been sent down from the sky. Focus your attention on this sphere of blue light. Then imagine it growing bigger and larger until it completely cocoons your home. This cocoon of light will protect your home during the hours you are asleep and when you are away at work.

Glossary

Affliction stars Negative symbols associated with Flying Star feng shui.

Arowana (dragon fish) A fish with silver scales and a swordlike body that is believed to bring good luck. It should have a healthy golden glow for maximum good fortune.

Astrology wheel A wheel showing the 12 animals of the Chinese Zodiac, which may be turned to align specific animals with the floor plan of a house.

Bright hall effect The effect created when there is an open space in front of the house, enabling beneficial chi to settle there before entering the home.

Chakras The seven main energy centers in the human body, which may be awakened by the seven colors of the rainbow.

Chi Lin A horse with a dragon head—a symbol that may be useful in business for promoting success and confidence.

Chinese prosperity coins Coins (ideally Chinese ones with a square hole in the center) that enhance good luck, especially if tied with a red cord and placed in a purse or wallet.

Chinese Zodiac An Eastern system of astrology in which 12 animals (the Rat, Ox, Tiger, Rabbit, Dragon, Snake, Horse, Monkey, Sheep, Rooster, Dog, and Pig) each represent one year in a 12-yearly cycle. Each animal is associated with a particular compass direction.

Compass feng shui/compass formula feng shui One of the two main schools of feng shui (the other being landscape feng shui), based on complex formulas associated with twenty-four directions (or the "twenty-four mountains") and requiring the use of a compass.

Cycles of relationships between the elements Three different cycles (producing cycle, exhausting cycle, destructive cycle) relating to the elements of wood, fire, earth, metal, and water. In the producing cycle: wood produces fire, which produces earth, which produce metal, which produces water, which produces wood, etc. In the exhausting cycle: fire exhausts wood, which exhausts water, which exhausts metal, which exhausts earth, which exhausts fire, etc. And in the destructive cycle: fire destroys metal, which destroys wood, which destroys earth, which destroys water, which destroys fire, etc.

Dragon-tortoise A powerful symbol with the body of a tortoise and the head of a dragon, and a baby tortoise on its back. It brings good luck in career and business.

Dragon and Phoenix symbol The ultimate yin and yang symbol, combining male strength and female beauty and representing happiness and success in marriage.

Eight aspirations method A method using the eight different types of luck associated with the eight sides of the Pa Kua. North symbolizes career aspirations; South fame aspirations; East health; West children; Northeast wisdom and literary aspirations; Northwest mentoring; Southeast wealth; and Southwest love and family.

Eight Mansions formula The formula by which everyone is either an East group or West group person; those in the East group should sleep in the East, North, South, and Southeast sectors; those in the West group in the West, Southwest, Northwest, and Northeast sectors.

Element cure method A method for curing feng shui ills using the elements.

Feng shui ruler A ruler (with dimensions in metric and imperial measurements) giving four sets of auspicious and four sets of inauspicious directions.

Five element colors The colors of blue, green, red, yellow, and white, corresponding to the five elements of water, wood, fire, earth, and metal.

Five element cycles The productive and destructive cycles in the relationships between the elements (see "cycles of relationships" above), in which certain color combinations manifest either good or bad luck.

Five Yellow A time-dimension affliction, which affects different compass areas in different years and brings with it ill luck. It may be counteracted by using various remedies or by leaving the relevant area undisturbed.

Five-element pagoda A remedy (best made of chrome or brass) that may be used to counteract the Five Yellow.

Flying Star feng shui A method of feng shui dealing with the time dimension and involving the casting of natal charts.

Fu dogs Symbolic guard dogs that offer protection against ill luck. Ideally a pair of Fu dogs should be placed high up on either side of a gate.

Fu wei direction The direction that should be faced for luck in examinations and interviews.

Fuk Luk Sau The three star gods of health, wealth, and happiness. Ideally they should be placed high up in the dining room.

Gem tree A version of the money tree, symbolizing wealth energy for the inhabitants of the home. Its leaves are made of semi-precious stones and its stems of gold.

Ho Tu square A pattern of numbers arranged so that all the even or all the odd numbers add up to twenty (excluding the central figure 5). The Ho Tu combinations of 1/6, 8/3, 7/2, and 4/9 are very auspicious, particularly for couples.

I Ching A classic text, also known as the Book of Changes, and the source of many of China's cultural practices. Its sixty-four hexagrams (six-lined symbols) offer predictions and warnings, as well as sound advice.

Karma Destiny, or the law of cause and effect, whereby a person's actions in their lifetime determine their fate.

KUA numbers Personalized numbers (based on gender and date of birth) that reveal favorable and unfavorable directions for individuals (see tip 107 for the method of working out your own KUA number).

Kuan Kung The god of wealth (based on Kuan Ti, the most famous general in Chinese history) and a powerful guardian. His image should ideally be placed in the Northwest corner of the home.

Kun A yin trigram symbolizing fertility and maternal qualities; its image is Big Earth.

Landscape feng shui The original classic school of feng shui, also known as form feng shui and based on the forms of the land.

Natal chart Charts that show the favorable "nine palaces," or auspicious sectors, of the home. They are best read in conjunction with annual Flying Star charts.

Nien yen direction One of the four lucky directions associated with each KUA number under the Eight Mansions formula. It is a favorable direction for love, family, and marriage.

Pa Kua An eight-sided image incorporating the symbols, directions, and numbers that are needed for feng shui analysis. The father should be in the Northwest corner of the house and the mother in the Southwest.

Pa Kua Eight Aspirations A school of feng shui whereby eight aspirations are associated with the eight sides of the Pa Kua.

Pa Kua mirror A defensive tool used to deflect poison arrows and absorb hostile energy.

Period 8 An earth period (representing the mountain) that began on February 4, 2004 and will finish on February 4, 2024. During this time academic research and meditation will be to the fore.

Poison arrows Hostile structures (such as long, straight roads that point at the door of your home; pointed roof lines; rocky outcrops; and pointed facades on nearby buildings) that emit negative energy. They may be overcome using element cures.

Primary directions The four cardinal points of the compass: North, South, East, and West.

Quarrelsome number 3 star The number 3 star is one of the problem "stars" in the Flying Star system. Each year, the number 3 star flies to different sectors of the home where it brings quarrelsome, hostile energy into the house. In 2007, the number 3 is located in the Northwest sector.

Ru Yi An image, also known as the scepter of office, used to increase authority and respect.

Secondary directions The four secondary points of the compass: Northwest, Southwest, Northeast, and Southeast.

Shar chi Killing energy that brings misfortune and represents the opposite of sheng chi. It may be caused by poison arrows or other factors.

Sheng chi Beneficial energy that brings good luck and represents the opposite of shar chi. It may be created by the surrounding landscape or by certain feng shui formulas.

Tai chi A series of exercises based on energizing chi within the body and on a balance of yin and yang meditation.

Three Killings An unlucky Flying Star feature, which occupies one of the four cardinal directions each year.

Three-legged toad A highly favorable money-making symbol, which will attract wealth luck to your home. It usually has three coins in its mouth and sits on a bed of coins.

Tien ti ren A trinity (heaven luck, earth luck, and human luck) that rules fortune and misfortune. One is born with heaven luck, but earth and human luck may both be manipulated.

Tien yi The direction that promotes good health, based on the Eight Mansions formula.

Trigrams The eight main symbols of feng shui analysis, which are positioned around the eight sides of the Pa Kua. They comprise three-lined combinations of broken and unbroken lines. The four most important ones are the Chien trigram (father), Kun trigram (mother), Ken trigram (son), and Sun trigram (daughter).

Tsai Shen Yeh A popular wealth god, usually shown sitting on a tiger, dressed in dragon robes and holding an ingot.

Water star 8/water star An auspicious symbol in Flying Star feng shui, symbolizing the luckiest location for water.

YANG Dwelling Classic An old feng shui text written during the Tang Dynasty that contained many feng shui rules on landforms and the environment.

Index

E

F

G

H

I

Useful websites

For further information about feng shui, visit Lillian Too's personal website or the World of Feng Shui website:

- http://www.lillian-too.com
- http://www.wofs.com